Rupert Brooke: A Memoir

Sir Edward Howard Marsh

RUPERT BROOKE

A MEMOIR

The
COLLECTED POEMS
of
RUPERT BROOKE

WITH A
PHOTOGRAVURE PORTRAIT
of the AUTHOR

Cloth, $1.25 net   Leather, $2.00 net

"It is packed with the stuff of which poetry
is made: vivid imagination, the phrase that
leaps to life, youth, music, and the ecstasy
born of their joy when genius keeps them company."—*The Outlook.*

JOHN LANE COMPANY
PUBLISHERS   NEW YORK

R U P E R T   B R O O K E

1913

RUPERT BROOKE
A MEMOIR

BY
EDWARD MARSH

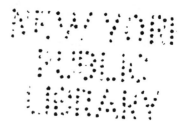
NEW YORK
JOHN LANE COMPANY
MCMXVIII

Copyright, 1918,
BY JOHN LANE COMPANY

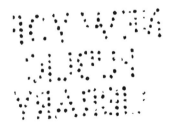

Press of
J. J. Little & Ives Company
New York, U. S. A.

INTRODUCTION

I FEEL that an apology is due to those who have been looking for some time for a Memoir of my son. The chief reason for the delay has been my great desire to gain the collaboration of some of his contemporaries at Cambridge and during his young manhood, for I believe strongly that they knew the largest part of him. Up to now it has been found impossible to do this, much as I should have wished it; and as since his death many of them have also laid down their lives, there is no longer any hope of doing so in the future. I have therefore consented to the Memoir coming out now, although it is of necessity incomplete. I cannot speak strongly enough of the ability and loving care that Mr. Marsh has given to the work.

M. R. B.

April, 1918

NOTE

THIS Memoir was written in August, 1915, a few months after Rupert Brooke's death, and my intention was to publish it with his collected poems in the course of that year. Circumstances prevented this, and now that three years have passed I ought probably to rewrite it in the changed perspective and on a different scale. As this is impossible for several reasons, I have had to be contented with a general revision, and the addition of letters which have since come into my hands.

I am very grateful to his Mother and to those of his friends who have allowed me to quote from his letters and from their accounts of him.

E. M.

April, 1918.

CONTENTS

RUPERT BROOKE

A MEMOIR

I

RUPERT BROOKE was born at Rugby on August 3rd, 1887. His father was William Parker Brooke, a Rugby master, son of Canon Brooke of Bath; and his mother was Mary Ruth Cotterill. He was the second of three brothers.[1]

When he was five years old his father became Housemaster of School Field, which was his home till 1910. He loved the house and the garden, especially his own particular long grass-path with borders and pergolas, where he used to walk up and down reading. At this House he entered Rugby in 1901, from the preparatory school at Hillbrow, and next year won a scholarship.

His school life was very happy. In his first

[1] Dick, who was six years older, died in 1907; and Alfred, three years younger, was killed near Vermelles in June, 1915, serving as a lieutenant in the Post Office Rifles.

year at Cambridge, reading out a paper on Modern Poetry which he had written at the end of his last term at Rugby for the School Society called Ἔρανος, and afraid that the alarming undergraduates might think it sentimental, he excused himself by explaining the circumstances in which he wrote it. "I had been happier at Rugby," he said, "than I can find words to say. As I looked back at five years, I seemed to see almost every hour golden and radiant, and always increasing in beauty as I grew more conscious; and I could not (and cannot) hope for or even quite imagine such happiness elsewhere. And then I found the last days of all this slipping by me, and with them the faces and places and life I loved, and I without power to stay them. I became for the first time conscious of transience, and parting, and a great many other things."

This happiness was compounded from many sources: friendship, games (he played for the School in both the XI and the XV), and books. He was a balanced combination of the athletic and the intellectual types of schoolboy—'always with a ball in his hand and a book in his pocket' is a vivid little description. "Rupert" (writes a contemporary in the VIth who was at another house, and afterwards became an Assistant Master [1]), "first of all people at school gave me an inkling of what a full life really meant. I was an awful Philistine, and still am, I fear; but he, with no appearance of superiority or attempt at preaching, as keen as any of us on all the immensely important events in school life, and always ready for a rag, impressed us as no one else could with the fact that these things were not all —not even the most important. And the best thing about him was that he was not out to impress us—it was just being himself."

His great school-friend Hugh Russell-Smith, since killed in action, wrote in the Rugby paper, the 'Meteor,' when he died:—

"For the first two or three years, I think, few of us realised that someone out of the ordinary had come among us. He was rather shy and quiet, though he at once proved himself a good athlete, and he lived much the same life as anyone else. Gradually, however, we began to notice little things about him. Instead of coming 'down town' with us, he used to go off to the Temple Library to read the reviews of books in the 'Morning Post' and 'Chronicle.' He read Walter Pater, and authors we knew very little about. He read a good deal of poetry, and he

[1] Hubert Podmore, who, before he was killed in action, gave Mrs. Brooke leave to publish this extract from his letter to her.

let us find him in raptures over Swinburne. He began to wear his hair rather longer than other people. Still, he played games enthusiastically, and helped us to become Cock House in football and in cricket. Gradually most of us in the House came under his spell. We accepted his literary interests. He was so straightforward and unaffected and natural about them, and he took our chaff so well, that we couldn't have helped doing so. Perhaps they amused most of us, but one or two—and those the most unlikely—were occasionally found clumsily trying to see what there really was in such things. But it was his personal charm that attracted us most, his very simple and lovable nature. Few could resist it. When in his last year he became head of the House, almost everyone came under the sway of his personality. It seems to me now, as it seemed then, that there really was a spirit in School Field which made it rather different from any other House. It was due, I believe, partly to Rupert, partly to his father. The situation might have been difficult for both. The way in which things actually turned out shows one of the most delightful sides of Rupert. He was in all things more than loyal to his father, but he never made it awkward for the rest of us. His sense of fun saw him through, and it helped us a good deal to know that he would not misinterpret all the little pleasantries that boys make at the expense of their Housemaster. The result was a sort of union between the Housemaster and the House, which made very much for good.

"Outside the House, his worth was realised to the full by some—by the Upper Bench, and by a few of the Masters who knew and loved him. He rose to a high place in the VIth, won two prizes for his poems, played cricket and football for the School, and became a Cadet Officer in the Corps. But I think he was never a school hero. It was chiefly his House that knew his lovableness. And when he was at Cambridge, I think he always loved the House lunches, which we used to have nearly every week. The last letter I had from him was one in which he was talking of members of the House who had fallen in the war.

"Rupert had an extraordinary vitality at school, which showed itself in a glorious enthusiasm and an almost boisterous sense of fun— qualities that are only too rare in combination. Of his enthusiasm it is hard to speak; we knew less about it, although we felt it. We knew much more of his glorious fooling—in his letters, in his inimitable and always kind burlesques of masters or boys, in his parodies of himself. He seemed almost always ready for laughter. It is often the small things that stand out most vividly in one's mind. I see Rupert singing at the very top of his voice, with a magnificent disregard for tune, the evening hymn we used to have so often at Bigside Prayers. I see him rushing on to the Close to release a sheep that had become entangled in one of the nets. I see him tearing across the grass so as not to be late for Chapel. I generally think of him with a book. He had not yet developed that love of the country and that passion for swimming with which the friends of his Grantchester days associate him. He used to read, when we used to walk or bathe. But whatever he was doing or wherever he was, he was always the same incomparable friend. He has often quoted to me a verse of Hilaire Belloc:

> From quiet homes and first beginning,
>   Out to the undiscovered ends,
> There's nothing worth the wear of winning,
>   But laughter and the love of friends.

How much Rupert loved Rugby while he was there, I know; and I know too how much those who knew him there loved him."

The letters which he wrote in his last year at school are radiant. "I am enjoying everything immensely at present. To be among 500 people, all young and laughing, is intensely delightful and interesting. . . .[1] I am seated on the topmost pinnacle of the Temple of Joy. Wonderful things are happening all around me. Some day when all the characters are dead—they are sure to die young—I shall put it all in a book. I am in the midst of a beautiful comedy—with a sense of latent tears—and the dramatic situations work out delightfully. The rest are only actors; I am actor and spectator as well, and I delight in contriving effective exits. The world is of gold and ivory. . . . How is London? Here the slushy roads, grey skies, and epidemic mumps cannot conceal a wonderful beauty in the air which makes New Big School almost bearable." And in the summer: "I am infinitely happy. I am writing nothing. I am content to live. After this term is over, the world awaits. But I do not now care what will come then. Only, my present happiness is so great that I fear the jealous gods will requite me afterwards with some terrible punishment, death perhaps —or life."

'Work' was only one of the lesser elements which went to make up all this joy. He got a

---

[1] Throughout this book, three dots mean that there are dots in the original letters; six, that something is omitted.

fair number of prizes, and went to King's with a scholarship: but lessons seem to have been almost the only thing he didn't as a rule care for. He would have liked to read the books as books, but grammar irked him. When he came to 'extra work' for the scholarship examination, he enjoyed it. "This introduces me to many authors whom the usual course neglects as 'unclassical.' . . . Theocritus almost compensates me for all the interminable dullness of Demosthenes and the grammars on other days. I never read him before. I am wildly, madly enchanted by him." He never became an accurate scholar, and though he enjoyed certain authors, and had a special love for Plato, I don't think Greek and Latin played the part in his development which might have been expected.

His voluntary reading, at school and afterwards, was mainly English—quantities of prose, but still more poetry, in which his taste was very comprehensive; and his zealous interest in contemporary work had already begun. A paper on Modern Poetry, which he read to the Ἔρανος Society, presses on his hearers Kipling, Henley, Watson, Yeats, A. E., and —— Ernest Dowson. This brings us to his amusing phase of 'decadence.' From 1905 till well into his second year at Cambridge he entertained a *culte* (in

such intensity, somewhat belated) for the literature that is now called 'ninetyish'—Pater,[1]
Wilde, and Dowson. This was a genuine enthusiasm, as anyone may see from his earliest
published work, especially the poems written in
the alexandrine of 'Cynara,' of which the 'Day
that I have loved' is the culmination. But he
loved to make fun of it, and of himself in it; for
all through his life his irony played first on himself. Here is the setting of a dialogue: "The
Close in a purple evening in June. The air is
full of the sound of cricket and the odour of the
sunset. On a green bank *Rupert* is lying. There
is a mauve cushion beneath his head, and in his
hand E. Dowson's collected poems, bound in pale
sorrowful green. He is clothed in indolence and
flannels. *Enter Arthur.*" 'Good-morrow,' says
Arthur. 'What a tremulous sunset!' But that
is all he is allowed to say. *Rupert* proceeds with
an elaborately 'jewelled' harangue, ending 'I
thank you for this conversation. You talk won-

[1] A little parody with which he won a Westminster Gazette prize
in 1907 may be worth preserving here: *"From 'Marius the Bank
Clerk,' by Walter Pater (Book II. Chap. ix., 'Procrastination').*
Well! it was there, as he beat upon the station gate (that so sym-
bolic barrier!) and watched the receding train, that the idea came
upon him; casting, as it were, a veil of annoyance over the vague
melancholy of his features; and filling, not without a certain
sedate charm, as of a well-known ritual, his mind with a now
familiar sense of loss—a very *desiderium*—a sense only momentarily perceptible, perhaps, among the other emotions and thoughts,
that swarmed, like silver doves, about his brain."

derfully. I love listening to epigrams. I wonder if the dead still delight in epigrams. I love to think of myself seated on the greyness of Lethe's banks, and showering ghosts of epigrams and shadowy paradoxes upon the assembled wan-eyed dead. We shall smile, a little wearily I think, remembering. . . . Farewell.' 'Farewell,' says poor *Arthur,* opening his mouth for the second time—and *exit.*

"I am busy with an enormous romance, of which I have written five chapters. It begins with my famous simile [1] about the moon, but soon gets much more lewd. One of the chief characters is a dropsical leper whose limbs and features have been absorbed in one vast soft paunch. He looks like a great human slug, and he croaks infamous little songs from a wee round mouth with yellow lips. The others are less respectable.

"Did you see the bowdlerised decadent?[2] I suppose the scenery looked extremely valuable. I dare not witness it. Nero is one of the few illusions I have left. All my others are departing one by one. I read a book recently which proved that Apollo was an aged Chieftain who lived in Afghanistan and had four wives and cancer in the stomach; and the other day I found

---

[1] This was as follows:—"The moon was like an enormous yellow scab on the livid flesh of some leper."

[2] *Nero* at His Majesty's Theatre.

myself—my last hope!—acting on moral prin-
ciples."

"This morning I woke with ophthalmia," he
wrote in another letter, "one of the many diseases raging through Rugby. It is all owing to
a divine mistake. I wanted to get rose-rash, being both attracted by the name and desirous to
have the disease over before the time of the Italian 'tour' came. Therefore yestre'en I prayed to
Æsculapius a beautiful prayer in Sapphics—it
began, I think, ἱμερος νῦν ἐστι ῥόδοις πυρέττειν, . . . but
either my Greek was unintelligible, or the names
of ills have changed since Æsculapius, for I
awoke and found the God had sent me this, the
least roseate of diseases."

He wished, of course, or rather wished to be
thought to wish, to shock and astonish the respectable; but he did not in practice go very far
in that diretcion. His hair, slightly longer than
usual, has already been mentioned. Ties might
not be coloured; but there was no rule against
their being 'puff' and made of *crêpe de chine;*
and such ties he wore, as did the other school
swells. It was amusing to cause a flutter in the
orthodox School Societies, of which he was really
an active and enthusiastic member, though one
might not think so from his accounts of their
proceedings. "Last Sunday I read a little paper

on *Atalanta,* and was mightily pleased. The usual papers we have are on such subjects as Hood or Calverley—'something to make you laugh.' . . . I saw my opportunity, and took it. 'Have I not,' I said, 'many a time and oft been bored beyond endurance by such Philistines? Now my revenge comes; I shall be merciless!' So I prepared a very long and profound paper, full of beautiful quotations, and read it to them for a long time, and they were greatly bored. They sat round in chairs and slumbered uneasily, moaning a little; while I in the centre ranted fragments of choruses and hurled epithets upon them. At length I ended with Meleager's last speech, and my voice was almost husky with tears; so that they woke, and wondered greatly, and sat up, and yawned, and entered into a discussion on *Tragedy,* wherein I advanced the most wild and heterodox and antinomian theories, and was very properly squashed. So, you see, even in Rugby the Philistines don't get in their own way always."

"I am finishing my paper on James Thomson.[1] I have cut out all the wicked parts, but I still fear for the reception. Last week we had a paper on T. Gray. The stupendous ass who wrote

---

[1] He had 'ransacked the eight bookshops in Charing Cross Road' for Thomson's works. (This is, of course, the author of the *City of Dreadful Night,* not of the *Seasons.*)

and read it, after referring to the Elegy as 'a fine lyric,' ended with the following incomparable words: 'In conclusion, we may give Gray a place among the greatest, above all, except perhaps Shakespeare, Milton, and Tennyson.' This lewd remark roused me from the carefully-studied pose of irritating and sublime nonchalance which I assume on such ocasions. I arose, and made acid and quite unfair criticisms of Gray and Tennyson, to the concealed delight of all the avowed Philistines there, and the open disgust of the professing 'lovers of literature.' I was nearly slain."

He wrote quantities of poetry at Rugby, a very little of which he thought worth preserving in the '1905-1908' section of his first book. Some of it appeared in the *Phœnix*, a free-lance school paper of which he was twin-editor, and some in the *Venture*, which succeeded the *Phœnix*. His verse of this time shows a good ear, and a love of 'beautiful' words, but not much else. A good deal of it was written when he ought to have been otherwise employed. "I shall sit in a gondola," he wrote when he was going to Venice in April, 1906, "and pour forth satires in heroic verse, or moral diatribes in blank verse. Intense surroundings always move me to write in an opposite vein. I gaze on the New Big School, and give utterance to frail diaphanous lyrics, sudden and beautiful as a rose-petal. And when I do an hour's 'work' with the Headmaster, I fill notebooks with erotic terrible fragments at which even Sappho would have blushed and trembled."

In 1904 he was given an extra prize for a poem on *The Pyramids,* and next year he won the real prize with one on *The Bastile,* which he recited on June 24th. "The speeches were rather amusing. I am informed that my effort was one of the only two audible; and as the other was in a foreign tongue, I carried off the honours. I am also told —by a cricketer friend of mine—that half the audience were moved to laughter, the other half to tears, which I regard as a compliment, though I can understand the feelings of neither half. Anyhow I got a Browning and a Rossetti out of it, which is something, though they *are* in prize-binding."

Next year he had to fall back on prose. "I have undertaken to write an Essay for a prize. If I win this I shall stand up next Speech Day and recite weird 'historical' platitudes to a vast slumbrous audience. The idea is so pleasingly incongruous that I desire to realize it. Moreover, I once airily told a pedantic and aged man that if I liked I could understand even History, and he, scoffing, stirred my pride to prove it. Therefore I am going to write an Essay on "The Influence of William III. on England.' Of William III. I know very little. He was a King, or something, they say, of the time of Congreve and Wycherley. Of England I know nothing. I thought you might aid me in a little matter like this. If ever you have written an epic, a monograph, an anthology, or a lyric on William III., please send it to me that I may quote it in full." He won the prize (the King's Medal for Prose); and as he got into the XI. at about the same time, he left Rugby with honours thick upon him.

II

His first year at King's (1906-7) was rather unsatisfactory. He regretted Rugby; and he was (as always) rather shy, and (for the first and only time) a little on the defensive with the strange people. The 'decadent' pose lingered; he had Aubrey Beardsleys in his room, sat up very late, and didn't get up in the morning. He thought it right to live entirely for the things of the mind; his passion for the country had not yet begun, and it seemed to him a wicked waste of time to walk or swim—two things which came soon afterwards to give him as much pleasure as anything in the world.

His letters are plaintive: "This place is rather funny to watch; and a little wearying. . . . At certain moments I perceive a pleasant kind of peace in the grey ancient walls and green lawns among which I live; a quietude that doesn't compensate for the things I have loved and left, but at times softens their outlines a little. If only I were a poet, I should love such a life very greatly, 'remembering moments of passion in tranquillity'; but being first and chiefly only a boy, I am restless and unable to read or write. . . . These people are often clever, and always wearying. The only persons I ever make any effort to see are two who came up with me from my House at Rugby. Here across the Styx we wander about together and talk of the upper world, and sometimes pretend we are children again."

He joined the A.D.C., and played *Stingo* in *She Stoops to Conquer;* but his chief public appearance in his first term was in the Greek play, the *Eumenides.* "The idea of my playing Hermes fell through," he wrote to his Mother, "but they have given me the equally large part of the Herald. I stand in the middle of the stage and pretend to blow a trumpet, while somebody in the wings makes a sudden noise. The part is not difficult." "I wear a red wig and cardboard armour," he wrote in another letter, "and luckily am only visible for a minute." It turned out that he was one of the successes of the evening. His radiant, youthful figure in gold and vivid red and blue, like a Page in the Riccardi Chapel, stood strangely out against the stuffy decorations and dresses which pervaded those somewhat palmy days of the Cambridge Theatre. After eleven years, the impression is still vivid.

At the beginning of next term his elder brother died suddenly. They were very fond of each other, and this was, I suppose, his first great sorrow. "It seems so strange that you haven't heard," he wrote. "I had thought that all the world must know. I suppose I ought to have written and told you; but there were so many letters to write; and I had to try to comfort Mother a little. Dick died on Sunday the 13th after a week's illness. Father was with him— but I don't think details matter much. . . . I came up here on Tuesday, partly to escape my Rugby school-friends, and partly that I might be alone."

"I'm rather wretched and ill," he writes a little later. "In my 'literary life' I have taken the last step of infamy, and become—a reviewer!

I've undertaken to 'do' great slabs of minor poetry for the *Cambridge Review*. I've read volumes of them, all the same, and all exactly the stuff *I* write. I often wonder whether I haven't written several of them myself under a pseudonym, and forgotten about it."

In his first Long Vacation,[1] "I work hundreds of hours a day," he writes, "at stuffy classics, and ooze with grammar. To save my soul, I write thousands of poems in the evening, and burn, them. I'll quote to you one verse of an immensely long one in six cantos, entitled 'A Song Illustrative of a Sense of Incompatibility between Self and Universe; also In Favour of Decease.'

> Things are beasts,
> Alas! and Alack!
> If life is a succession of choreic anapæsts,
> When, ah! when shall we arrive at the Parœmiac?"

Part of this Long was spent at Lulworth, where he wrote to his Mother: "One day we were reading on the rocks, and I had a Keats in my pocket, and it slipped out, and, falling into a swift current, was borne out to sea. So we leapt into a boat and rowed up and down the coast

---

[1] I may as well mention that I first met him just after the end of the May Term this year. After this I saw him at intervals, and we knew each other pretty well by the summer of 1909.

till we espied it off some rocks. But the sea was rather rough and we could not land on that rocky part, or get near Keats. So we landed half a mile off on a beach, and came over the rocks to the Keats; and when we found it, I stripped and went in after it and got it. It is indeed quite spoilt; but it only cost two shillings to begin with." (He did not know at this time of an association which he discovered four years afterwards. "Oh, I've read Keats," he writes in 1911, "and found the most AMAZING thing. The last place he was in was Lulworth. His ship was becalmed outside. He and Severn went ashore and clambered about the rocks all day—his last fairly happy day. He went aboard and wrote, that evening, his last poem—that sonnet. The ship took him on to Italy, coughing blood and suffering Hell because he wouldn't see Fanny any more. Fanny sat in Hampstead, with Mr. Brown. It was at the end of Sept. 1820 . . .")

There is a gloomy letter of the day after his birthday, when he became twenty. "I am now in the depths of despondency because of my age. I'm filled with an hysterical despair to think of fifty dull years more. I hate myself and everyone. I've written almost no verse for ages; and shall never write any more. I've forgotten all rhythm and metre. The words 'anapæstic dimeter

acatalectic,' that fired me once, now leave me cold.
The sunset or a child's face no longer reminds me
of a bucolic cæsura. But I still read plaintively,
to pass the time." And he can still write at the
end of this Long: "Go back to Cambridge for
my second year and laugh and talk with those
old dull people on that airless plain! The
thought fills me with hideous *ennui.*"

But this mood was already something of a literary survival, and well understood to be so by
his friends. He went back to games, especially
football; and by the beginning of his second year
he had become one of the most interested and interesting people at Cambridge.

> A young Apollo, golden-haired,
>   Stands dreaming on the verge of strife,
> Magnificently unprepared
>   For the long littleness of life.

Mrs. Cornford's epigram on him is well known,
but one could not write about his great days at
Cambridge without quoting it—bitter though the
irony of 'long' has now become.

Henceforward friends and avocations crowded
on him. He had been the chief advocate of the
Labour Party at Rugby; and at King's he joined
various societies, political and intellectual, mostly
more or less revolutionary—the University

Fabian Society, of which he became President for the year 1909-10; the Carbonari; and the Heretics. He also belonged to that old, great, secret, but vaguely famous Brotherhood from which the membership of Tennyson and others of the illustrious has lifted a corner of the veil. J. T. Sheppard, Fellow of King's, gives an account of some among these activities. "The Carbonari, I think, he founded; a Society which, in spite of its terrifying name, was very friendly. The paper and the talk which followed it at the one meeting to which, as an elderly person, I was allowed admission, were frank and amusing, but my chief memory is of the cheerful kindliness of the members. Then there were the Fabians, whom he sometimes entertained to a frugal supper of bread and cheese and beer in his rooms, and to whom he never tired of teaching the importance of poets and artists in the good society which is to be built up by our children. His advice to the State was very practical. Since poets and artists matter, and since they need time for development, we, who are not the poets and the artists, ought to organise the material requisites, bread and cheese and leisure, for those who seem to show the promise of good work. He believed that you do not improve a poet by starving and neglecting him; and one good way of showing that we remember him would be to remember also that it is our duty to buy as well as read the works of the poets who are still writing."

Rupert indeed wore his Socialism with a difference, which comes out in a letter of December, 1907, thanking his uncle, Mr. Clement Cotterill, for his book, *Human Justice for those at the Bottom,* in which he says that he has been urging his Socialist friends at Cambridge, especially the Fabians, to take a more human view of things. "Socialism is making great advances at Oxford and Cambridge just now; but its upholders are too apt to make it seem, to others and to themselves, a selfish scheme of economics. They confound the means with the end; and think that a Compulsory Living Wage is the end, instead of a good beginning. Bernard Shaw came down last term, and made a speech that was enthusiastically received, in which he advised a state of things in which each 'class' had its own party in Parliament fighting for its own hand. The whole thing was based on selfishness. It was not inspiring.

"Of course they're really sincere, energetic, useful people, and they do a lot of good work. But, as I've said, they're rather hard. Must every cause lose part of its ideal, as it becomes successful? And also they are rather intolerant, especially towards the old order. They some-

times seem to take it for granted that all rich
men, and all Conservatives (and most ordinary
Liberals) are heartless villains. I have already,
thanks, in part, to some words of yours, got some
faith in the real, sometimes overgrown, goodness
of all men; and that is why I have found your
book so good, as a confirmation rather than a
revelation. And this faith I have tried to ham-
mer into those Socialists of my generation whom
I have come across. But it's sometimes hard.
The prejudices of the clever are harder to kill
than those of the dull. Also I sometimes wonder whether this Commercialism, or Competition,
or whatever the filthy infection is, hasn't spread
almost too far, and whether the best hope isn't
in some kind of upheaval."

All this is supplemented in an account written
by Hugh Dalton, an intimate friend of this time.
"During our years at Cambridge, Fabianism was
at its high tide, and attracted most of those who
had any social enthusiasm worth speaking of.
Rupert joined the C.U.F.S. in April, 1907. He
came to me, I remember, and said, 'I'm not your
sort of Socialist; I'm a William Morris sort of
Socialist, but I want to join your Society as an
Associate.' He became a full member a year
later. Like many of us, he was falling by then
under the subtle influence of the Webbs, and

simultaneously the atmosphere of Cambridge was teaching him to value and to cultivate lucidity of thought and precision of reasoning. He soon saw the intellectual limitations of a 'William Morris sort of Socialist,' and though he never studied the fine points of economics, he came to talk very good sense on the larger economic questions.

"It was through the meetings of the *Carbonari* that I first came to know him well. This was a society of our contemporaries in King's, about a dozen, which we formed in our first term for papers and discussions. Rupert and I and one or two others were generally the last to separate, and sometimes the dawn was in the sky before we got to bed. We walked round the Courts and beside the river for hours, trying to get things clear. For we wanted, half passionately and half humorously, to get everything clear quickly. Hitherto, we thought, we had been too young to think, and soon we might be too busy, and ultimately we should be too old. The golden time was now.

" 'There are only three things in the world,' he said once, vehemently answering some Carbonaro who had been talking like a Philistine, 'one is to read poetry, another is to write poetry, and the best of all is to live poetry!' And I remember his saying that at rare moments he had glimpses of what poetry really meant, how it solved all problems of conduct and settled all questions of values. Moreover, it kept men young, he thought. One night we were sitting at a high window overlooking King's Parade. We had been discussing some philosophical point about the nature of Beauty, when we saw and heard some drunken members of another college going home. 'Those fellows,' he said, 'would think us very old if they had been in this room to-night, but when they go down and sit on office stools, *they* will grow old quite suddenly, and many years hence *we* shall still be talking and thinking about these sorts of things, and we shall still be young.'

"As for philosophy, he shared the general view of the set in which we moved that ethics were exceedingly important, but metaphysics rather trivial; that it mattered immensely what was good, but comparatively little what was real. I remember several fierce arguments [1] as to whether a man's character, as distinct from the series of states of mind through which he passed, could be good in itself, and also a controversy as to whether states of affairs, as distinct from the states of mind of the persons concerned in them, could be good in themselves. Rupert maintained that

[1] *Argument*, it will be remembered, at Youth's Funeral, was 'too full of woe to speak.'

Variety was good in itself. 'A world containing you and me and Maynard Keynes,' he said,
'is obviously better than a world containing three
people exactly like any one of us!'"

One of the most significant and absorbing of
his activities was the dramatic. Here I must
quote from E. J. Dent's admirable record:
"When I came back to Cambridge in the autumn
of 1907, I soon became aware that a new spirit
was making itself felt. Probably it was active
in more ways than I was able to observe; but
the first notable result of it was the performance of Marlowe's *Faustus* in November by a
number of men who afterwards constituted
themselves as the Marlowe Dramatic Society.
The new spirit seemed to come partly from
Rugby, partly from Bedales, and by an odd co-
incidence the two leaders, though not related,
bore the same name: Rupert and Justin Brooke.
It was a queer performance. The elder generation were scandalised almost before the play began: no scenery, only dingy green hangings, no
music, no footlights, frequent 'black-outs,' no
names of the actors printed. And all this in the
A.D.C. Theatre, with its familiar portraits, its
familiar memories! No wonder they were upset
by it all. '*Faustus* isn't a play at all'—'absurd

for undergraduates to attempt tragedy'—'why didn't they get somebody with experience to coach them?'—'why do they act in the dark?'— 'not always in very nice taste.' It was indeed a queer performance. Faustus looked absurdly young; Mephistopheles (Rupert), his face completely hidden by his cowl, generally turned his back to the audience, and spoke in a thick indistinct voice which often served merely as a background to the piercing whispers of the Master of ——, whose thirst for information was insatiable. But in spite of these things and many others, in spite of the tedious humour of the comic scenes, the play had a new spirit of its own. The tragic moments were genuinely moving. Crude, awkward, and amateurish as it all was, there was the spirit of true poetry about it. One felt that to these actors poetry was the greatest thing in life.

"The Marlowe group were inclined to be suspicious, perhaps not unjustly, of anyone who was a member of the Senate. But as I had been one of the few to admit themselves sincerely impressed by *Faustus*, I was occasionally allowed to hear news of their next project. Milton was to be commemorated in the summer,[1] and the young

[1] By this time the Authorities had come round to the Marlowe Society, and Christ's College bespoke a special performance of its *Comus* for their celebration of the Tercentenary.

poets were going to have a hand in it. Rupert was to be seen almost daily, I believe, in Room Theta, studying vast books on theatre-construction; a kind friend brought out for him his copy of the Trinity Milton facsimile, for the settling of points of textual criticism; and mysterious designs for costumes and scenery were handed round, in which wonderful effects *à la* Gordon Craig were to be obtained with scaffold poles.

"It is difficult to criticise *Comus,* or to write the history of its preparation. It had much the same faults and the same merits as *Faustus,* though on a larger scale. Rupert was not a good actor,[1] nor even a good speaker of verse. Yet I feel now that anyone who remembers *Comus,* and remembers it with ever so slight a sense of beauty, will think of Rupert as the central figure of it; and watching rehearsals daily, as I did, I felt that, however much his personal beauty might count for, it was his passionate devotion to the spirit of poetry that really gave *Comus* its peculiar and indescribable atmosphere.

"*Comus,* however unimportant to the world at large, did, in fact, mean a great deal for Rupert and his friends. It was the first time that he had

---

[1] He took the part of the Attendant Spirit. It is only fair to say that this view of his acting, or at any rate of his elocution, was far from universal.

had to bear the responsibility of a large undertaking, and he addressed himself to it in the spirit of a scholar. It deepened his sense of poetry, of drama, and of music; it made him develop an ideal continually present in his mind, even in later years, which gave solidity to his group, the ideal of Cambridge, of young Cambridge, as the source from which the most vital movements in literature, art, and drama, were to spring. *Comus* effected an intimate collaboration of all sorts of brains, and it effected especially a co-operation of men and women. Rupert was by no means the only remarkable person in the circle. He had, moreover, a power of making friends with women as well as with men, and although *Comus* was probably a symptom rather than a cause, it was from about that time that joint societies, such as the Heretics and the Fabians, began to make a new influence felt."

Rupert was knocked up by his exertions over *Comus*. He wrote from Rugby to Mrs. Cornford (then Miss Frances Darwin): "I went off without even saying good-bye or thank-you to people. My mother (I can plead) packed me up and snatched me here to sleep and recover. I am now convalescent, and can sit up and take a little warm milk-and-Tennyson. I feel a deserter; but I can always adduce the week when the Committee went to the seaside, and I faced the world and Albert's Artistic Temperament alone." [1]

He had written to his mother about this week, and about another matter. "Albert [Rutherston], who is painting our scenery, is staying with me. We paint in the theatre, 9 to 5 every day. I daub a little, but most of the time carry and empty pails, run errands, wind pulleys, etc. . . . I suppose you heard of the dreadful tragedy that happened last Saturday week—[Walter] Headlam's death? It was terribly sudden. He was about in King's all the week—kept the procession for the Chancellor's installation on Wednesday waiting for half an hour by being late—in his usual way! On Friday he was in King's, about, as usual. Friday evening he went up to town, had a slight operation (by some accounts), and died on Saturday morning. . . . It made me quite miserable and ill for some days. One gets so *angry* at that sort of thing. I didn't know him *very* well. But he was the one classic I really admired and liked;[2] and I had done a good deal of work with him. The papers made very little of it. He published so little that outside people

---

[1] It was at about this time that he bought two drawings by Augustus John, "very splendid ones—even the critical Albert admitted that, and confessed jealousy."

[2] It was not till later that he knew A. W. Verrall, whom he 'admired and liked' very much.

didn't know much of him. But his friends, and
we who were his pupils, knew his great genius.
I don't know how much of him they will be able
to rake together from his papers. But all the
great, ripe, splendid works we all proudly looked
forward to him achieving—which we knew he
might consummate any time he gave himself a
few months, have died with him: can never be
made. That's the terrible thing. Even in Cambridge many people knew of him most as a brilliant 'scholar,' *i. e.*, emender of Greek texts. But
he was also about the best writer of Greek there
has been since the Greeks. And what I loved so in
him was his extraordinary and living appreciation of all English poetry, modern and ancient.
To hear him repeat it was a delight. He was an
excellent poet himself, and had perfect taste. He
first inspired me with a desire to get *Comus* done,
a term or two ago, and has often talked about it
since. I had made up, in my mind, a little list
of things about which I was going to ask him,
large and small points, to make certain that we
should interpret and understand it in the best
way possible; but I put it off till too late. . . .
The whole thing makes me so rebellious—to think
what the world has lost."

· · · · · · ·

The vacations were spent in all sorts of ways: at the Fabian Summer School, or camping out with smaller groups of friends; on walking tours; or, at Christmas, with large heterogeneous parties for winter-sports in Switzerland. He told his mother of his plans for one of the Swiss excursions in the winter of 1908. "What I meant about the holidays is this. It is quite true that I have plenty of opportunities of resting. But I always feel that I oughtn't to, and can't, do nothing. There are so many things I must learn and do, and there is not too much time. My brain *must* be working. And so the only way (I find) I have a real holiday from my work, is on a walking-tour, or in Switzerland; times and places where it is impossible to think or read for more than five minutes. In a way such things are a waste of time. And I can't imagine anything I should hate more than a long 'holiday' like that, of more than a week or ten days. It would be intolerable. But, I think, just a week's mental rest strengthens a mind for some time. This sounds rather priggish; but I'm really very much in earnest about reading and writing."

The Swiss relaxations used to include the performance of a play, or even an opera—the *Importance of Being Earnest,* in which Rupert played Algernon, or a nonsense-melodrama written in collaboration by the party, but mostly by him. In the opera he was obliged at the last moment, by the sudden defection of the tenor, to play the hero. He couldn't sing a note; and the difficulty was got over by making the actor who played his valet stand beside him in a rigid position and sing, while Rupert did the gestures.

The English holidays were more peaceful. "Overcote is a lovely place," he wrote to his mother on one of them, "with nothing but an old inn, and a ferry. There are villages round, a mile or two away, but hidden. And there's just the Ouse, a slow stream, and some trees and fields, and an immense expanse of sky. There were a lot of wild birds about, wild duck, and snipe, and herons."

All these occasions produced floods of doggerel, some of which is amusing—from a snatch of blank verse on an unfortunate town-bred friend who arrived late on a wet night at a camp where all the beds were occupied, and didn't rise to the occasion:

> In the late evening he was out of place,
> And infinitely irrelevant at dawn,

—to the following elaborate ballade, composed
during a sleepless night when he and Dudley
Ward,[1] coming very late into Cranborne, couldn't
find the inn which they had picked out in the
guide-book for the sake of its name:

In Cranborne town two inns there are,
  And one the Fleur-de-Lys is hight,
And one, the inn Victoria,[2]
  Where, for it was alone in sight,
  We turned in tired and tearful plight
Seeking for warmth, and company,
  And food, and beds so soft and white—
These things are at the Fleur-de-Lys.

Where is the ointment for the scar?
  Slippers? and table deftly dight?
Sofas? tobacco? soap? and ah!
  Hot water for a weary wight?
  Where is the food, in toil's despite?
The golden eggs? the toast? the tea?
  The maid so pretty and polite?
These things are at the Fleur-de-Lys.

Oh, we have wandered far and far,
  We are fordone and wearied quite.
No lamp is lit; there is no star.
  Only we know that in the night
  We somewhere missed the faces bright,

---

[1] A Cambridge friend, not to be confused with the Member of
Parliament of the same name.
[2] Showing that a Grantchester man can make cockney rhymes
just like a Barton man.

The lips and eyes we longed to see;
   And Love, and Laughter, and Delight.
These things are at the Fleur-de-Lys.

Prince, it is dark to left and right.
   Waits there an inn for you and me?
Fine noppy ale and red firelight?
   These things are at the Fleur-de-Lys.

The next was written at a very favourite inn, the *Pink and Lily,* near Prince's Risborough, on one occasion when he went there with Jacques Raverat.

Never came there to the Pink
Two such men as we, I think.
Never came there to the Lily
Two men quite so richly silly;[1]
So broad, so supple, and so tall,
So modest and so brave withal,
With hearts so clear, such noble eyes,
Filled with such sage philosophies,
Thirsty for Good, secure of Truth,
Fired by a purer flame than youth,
Serene as age, but not so dirty,
Old, young, mature, being under thirty.
Were ever two so fierce and strong,
Who drank so deep, and laughed so long,
So proudly meek, so humbly proud,
Who walked so far, and sang so loud?

[1] This couplet, which is inconsistent with the rest, was supplied by his companion.

The last I will quote was pinned to some food which they left by the roadside after luncheon:

> Two men left this bread and cake
> For whomsoever finds to take.
> He and they will soon be dead.
> Pray for them that left this bread.

∙   ∙   ∙   ∙   ∙   ∙

From this time the story shall be told as far as possible in extracts from Rupert Brooke's letters to his friends, from which his character will appear far more vividly, and on the whole more clearly, than from anything that could be written about it. But the picture thus given must for various reasons be incomplete, and perhaps misleading; and a few touches must here be added, to be borne in mind while the letters are read.

They might, for instance, give the idea of self-absorption. Self-conscious he was, self-examining, and self-critical, to the last degree; but hardly ever self-absorbed. The extracts cannot show his continual helpfulness and serviceableness to his friends, both in large matters which are too private, and in details which are too trivial, to be chronicled. "There was a deep-seated generosity in him," says Mrs. Cornford, "at once sensible and tender. I used to think that the real reason the charm of his face struck peo-

ple so greatly was because its clearness and fair-
ness were not simply a happy accident of youth,
but expressed this innate quality in him. . . . He
was endlessly kind in helping me with my verses
(except that kindness seems the wrong word, because he did it as a matter of course). He would
sit for an hour or two at a time, generally on the
ground, frowning and biting the end of his pencil
and scribbling little notes on the margin before
we talked. Of the better things he would only
say 'I like that,' or 'That's good.' I can't imagine
him using a word of that emotional jargon in
which people usually talk or write of poetry. He
made it feel more like carpentering." Here we
see him as he often was, just simple and serious,
full of the business of the moment. Indeed he
was very restful to be with. The eager, working, excited brain which shows in the letters, incessantly registering, assimilating, juggling with,
sensations and impressions, hid its thrills under
an appearance almost of placidity. He never
'put himself forward,' and seldom took the lead,
in conversation; someone spoke of 'the beauty of
his eyes looking steadily and without mocking
into quite ordinary talk.' But he was 'noticing'
all the time; he had the power which women are
supposed to have of knowing everything that is

going on in the room; and he seemed never to forget the smallest detail.

His observation was always, if not 'mocking,' at any rate amused; and something must be said about the peculiar quality of his irony and his humour, which were very intimate, and might be misunderstood by strangers. J. T. Sheppard has written admirably about them, as they played on his friends. "He would laugh at them, and sometimes treat their most cherished enthusiasms as amusing, if harmless foibles; but he had not the power, possessed by some people who matter less, of making you seem small and dull. His society was, in the good sense, comfortable. He loved children, and when he treated his grown-up friends as rather absurd but very nice children, they would have had to be very absurd indeed to resent it. It must have been very hard to be pompous or priggish in his company." He treated himself in much the same way. If there was any fun to be got out of a laugh against him, far from grudging it, he gave every facility; but he liked to have the first go at it himself. There was always some foundation for the jokes; but the truth and the fun were inextricably mixed up, and one had to know exactly how many grains of salt to take. As an obvious instance: it was certainly his usual belief that he was, or at any

rate had it in him to be, a good poet; and so he
would describe himself as the first poet of the
age, because it *would* be funny if he thought so,
and therefore it was amusing to say so; and there
was no risk of his correspondents thinking him
cocksure. In the same way he would pick out his
best lines for special praise. "There's one *superb*
line," he said to me when he first showed me the
sonnet *Love*. " 'Astonishment is no more in hand
or shoulder.' Isn't it amazing?" He did think
it good, and was enjoying what Keats calls 'the
reperception and ratification of what is fine' in
his own work; but he said it with a twinkle.

He always loved to dramatise a situation, and
to make out that he had said or done something
absurdly striking and stunning. Here is a good
illustration from a letter of 1909: "And so I
walked and laughed and met a many people and
made a thousand songs—all very good—and, in
the end of the days, came to a woman who was
more glorious than the sun, and stronger and
stranger than the sea, and kinder than the earth,
who is a flower made out of fire, a star that laughs
all day, whose brain is clean and clear like a man's,
and her heart is full of courage and kindness; and
whom I love. I told her that the Earth was
crowned with windflowers, and dancing down the
violet ways of Spring; that Christ had died and

Pan was risen; that her mouth was like the sunlight on a gull's wings. As a matter of fact I believe I said 'Hullo! isn't it rippin' weather?' "

"You are the only person, Frances," he wrote much later to Mrs. Cornford, "who ever believed *all* my lies. Nothing (short, perhaps, of incredulity) can shake my devotion to you."

One more quotation from Sheppard: "He was kind and unaffected. But he was not miraculously unselfish, nor indifferent to his popularity. The fact that in small things he sometimes seemed to choose the pleasant second-best, and, as he himself realised, rather eagerly to accept the little successes which he could so easily win, should make us appreciate not less, but more, the rightness and the goodness of his larger choices. He was very sensitive to praise, and it would be wrong to say that he was always wisely praised. But he was sensible enough and strong enough to take flattery, in the long run, for what it was worth; and he valued the affection that was critical, not flattering.

"Because he was human, he enjoyed his popularity. The quality which won it was, I think, his power of liking people, and making them feel, because he liked them all, not only at their ease with him, but also happy and friendly with one another. His company had this effect at home, and in his rooms at King's, in his garden at Grantchester, in London, and I am sure wherever he went in Germany and in America. Certainly the most varied people used to delight in it, and he, for his part, was delighted when some of the incongruous persons he liked, unexpectedly also liked one another.

"He was in some ways like a child, very frank and simple, generally knowing what he wanted, and, if he could see it, taking it; but also, where his affections were concerned, most loyal and devoted; suffering acutely in the few great troubles that came to him, but generally confident and happy; above all delighting, and making other people share his delight, in a great number of different things."

III

He took the Classical Tripos in the summer of 1909, only getting a Second. This was a 'disappointment,' though not specially so to him. "He found English literature, now, for him, more important than the ancient classics; and he has convinced us all that he was right," says Sheppard, himself a Don at King's; so there is no need for head-shaking.

After term, he went to live within easy dis-

tance of Cambridge, at a house in Grantchester
called the Orchard.   Here he spent most of the
rest of this year, going for the summer holidays
to a vicarage his parents had taken at Clevedon
in Somerset, which he was allowed to cram with
relays of his friends.   He was working all these
months for the Charles Oldham Shakespeare
prize, which he won in the course of the Michael-
mas Term.

He went to Switzerland for Christmas, where
he got poisoned by drinking some bad water; and
he came home to find his father seriously ill with
hemorrhage on the brain.   He had to give up
Grantchester and Cambridge and all his plans
for next term, and undertake the temporary
management of the House at Rugby.   He wrote
to Mrs. Cornford to apologise for backing out of
his part in *The Land of Heart's Desire.*   "There
are other things I'm very sick to miss," he went
on: "the Marlowe play, and Verrall's lectures,
etc.—seeing you all—the whole life of it, in fact.
Also I fear I may have confused the Fabians
rather by not coming up.   I'm a general nuisance.
Oh! and I'm so sad and fierce and miserable not
to be in my garden and little house at Grantchester all this term.   I love being there so much
—more than any place I've ever lived in.   I love
the place and especially the solitude so much.   I'd

thought of being there when the spring was coming, every day this winter, and dreamt of seeing all the little brown and green things. It's horrible of me to talk like this when I'm in the house with two other people who are infinitely worse off in happiness than I am, and one of them in pain. . . . Many thanks for your letter, by the way. It cheered me greatly at the exact time when I was sitting gloomily waiting for my father's return from the London doctor, and wondering what the verdict would be. I had sunk into that abysmal darkness which comes on a convalescent when anything goes wrong. I've shaken off my dreadful disease now. It inspired me with thousands of Hardyesque short poems about people whose affairs went dismally wrong, or frightfully detestable people I couldn't help falling in love with, or interviews with the Almighty in which He turned out to be an absolute and unimaginative idiot. . . . But I hope to occupy my exile by composing some work of immortal genius."

A little later Mr. Brooke died suddenly, and was buried on the very day when the fifty boys were coming back to School Field. The shock was great. Rupert wrote to me in March, thanking me for a letter, "and indeed for the earlier ones to an invalid—though those seem so long ago that I cannot find continuity between that time and this. It is the smallest part of the gulf that I have been ill again—I collapsed, unforgivably [with influenza], just after the funeral; and again subsisted for days on milk and the pieces I could surreptitiously bite out of the end of my thermometer. Now, and lately, though, I am well and bursting with activity. I work like a Professor, and feel the Spring in my bones. I am acting Housemaster in my father's place till the end of the term. Then we are to be turned from this place by cold strangers, into a little house with a patch of grass in front, on a road, stiff and ugly. . . . I find I am an admirable schoolmaster. I have a bluff Christian tone that is wholly pedagogic. Also, they remember I used to play for the School at various violent games, and respect me accordingly."

"My heart is warm," he wrote to Jacques Raverat, "and has been half secure—or confident, rather—throughout the last four centuries (just a month) because of the splendid people I know. Half are scattered abroad now. But you'll all meet in April. I'll find all of you by August."

Some of them he did meet in April, when he wrote to me from Lulworth: "At length I am escaped from the world's great snare. This is heaven. Downs, Hens, Cottages, and the Sun.

. . . For the rest of Eternity my stabile address is 24 Bilton Road, Rugby. School Field, that palatial building, will know us no more. And henceforth I shall have to play on other people's tennis lawns. I wept copiously last week on saying good-bye to the three and fifty little boys whose Faith and Morals I had upheld for ten weeks. I found I had fallen in love with them all. They were so pleasant and fresh-minded as they were. And it filled me with purpureal gloom to know that their plastic souls would harden into the required shapes, and they would go to swell the indistinguishable masses who fill Trinity Hall, Clare, Caius . . . and at last become members of the English Upper, or Upper Middle, Classes. I am glad I am not going to be a schoolmaster for ever. The tragedy would be too great."

He went back to Grantchester for most of the May term, and immediately got caught up again in the multiplicity of Cambridge life. "I'm afraid there isn't the ghost of a chance," he wrote in answer to a suggestion that we should go abroad together for a fortnight. "I'm so extraordinarily inextricable and necessary! You think this conceit; but it's not. Various bodies and societies have arranged things in which I am continuously and hopelessly involved. Also my labours at the

University Library press most insistently upon me. I wish I could have come, it would have been lovely. Grantchester's lovely though, too. When are you coming? The apple-blossom and the river and the sunsets have combined to make me relapse into a more than Wordsworthian communion with nature, which prevents me reading more than 100 lines a day, or thinking at all."

His work at this time was on the Elizabethan drama, mainly for a monograph on 'Puritanism as represented or referred to in the early English drama up to 1642,' with which he won the Harness Prize this year.[1] It shows deep reading. "I read 20 pre-Elizabethan plays a week, all poor," he had written in March; and in April from Lulworth, "All the morning I souse myself in Elizabethan plays; and every afternoon I walk up perpendicular places alone, for hours"— adding in a moment of surfeit, "There are no good plays between 1500 and 1650, except the *Faithful Shepherdess*—and, perhaps, *Antony and Cleopatra.*"

By this time he had already written a good many of the poems which were to appear in the 1908-1911 section of his first book, and he was writing more. "I am slowly recovering from

[1] A copy of this essay is in the British Museum Library.

Work," he wrote to Mrs. Cornford. "Henceforth I am going to lead what Dudley calls 'a Life Dedicated to Art.' Hurray!" Mrs. Cornford and he both had plans for publishing a volume of poems in 1910—(hers was carried out, his postponed). "They will review us together!" he told her. "The *Daily Chronicle,* or some such, that reviews verse in lumps, will notice thirty-four minor poets in one day, ending with *Thoughts in Verse on many Occasions, by a Person of Great Sensibility,* by F. Cornford, and *Dead Pansy-Leaves, and other Flowerets,* by R. Brooke; and it will say, 'Mr. Cornford has some pretty thoughts; but Miss Brooke is always intolerable' (they always guess the sex wrong). And then I shall refuse to call on you. Or another paper will say, 'Major Cornford and the Widow Brooke are both bad; but Major Cornford is the worst.' And then you will cut me in the street."

The Marlowe Society's second performance of *Dr. Faustus,* got up for a party of fifty German students who visited Cambridge in August, was one excitement of this summer; and another was a tour with Dudley Ward in a disreputable-looking caravan, to popularise the Minority Report on the Poor Law in the principal towns on the South Coast—except Bournemouth, through which they drove, bare-headed and barefoot, at full speed, in fear or hope of being seen by a Conservative aunt who lived there.

Next month he wrote to F. H. Keeling [1] from Rugby. The letter is dated September 20th-28rd, 1910: "I've several times started to write you a notable and rhetorical letter, but my life has been too jerky to admit of much connected thought lately, so the letter always fizzled away, and was not. I'm sorry I didn't write sooner, but I wanted to be able to write down a great attack on your pessimism in abundant and reasoned language. And such a thing takes time and thought. Also, I may agree with you.

"What is pessimism? Why do you say you are becoming a pessimist? What does it mean? He may (I say to myself) mean that he thinks that the Universe is bad as a whole, or that it's bad just now, or that, more locally and importantly, things aren't going to get any better in our time and our country, no matter how much we preach Socialism and clean hearts at them.

"Is it the last two? Are you telling us that the world is, after all, bad, and, what's more horrible, without enough seeds of good in it? I, writing

---

[1] F. H. Keeling, or as he was always called by his friends, 'Ben' Keeling, the chief figure among the Cambridge Fabians of Rupert's day, was killed in the Somme Battle of 1916.

poetry and reading books and living at Grantchester all day, feel rather doubtful and ignorant
about 'the world'—about England, and men, and
what they're like. Still, I see some, besides the
University gang. I see all these queer provincials in this town, upper and middle and lower
class, and God knows they're sterile enough.

"But I feel a placid and healthy physician
about it all (only I don't know what drugs to
recommend). This is because I've such an over-
flowing (if intermittent) flood of anti-pessimism
in me. I'm using the word now in what I expect
is its most important sense, of a feeling rather
than a reasoned belief. The horror is not in
believing the Universe is bad—or even believing
the world won't improve—on a reasoned and cool
examination of all facts, tendencies and values,
so much as in a sort of general *feeling* that there
isn't much potentiality for good in the world, and
that anyhow it's a fairly dreary business,—an
absence of much appreciation and hope, and a
somehow paralysed will for good. As this is a
feeling, it *may* be caused by reason and experience, or more often by loneliness or soul-measles
or indigestion or age or anything else. And it
can equally be cured by other things than reason
—by energy or weather or good people, as well
as by a wider ethical grasp. At least, so I've

found in the rather slight and temporary fits of depression I've had, in exile or otherwise, lately —or even in an enormous period of Youthful Tragedy with which I started at Cambridge. I have a remedy. It is a dangerous one, but I think very good on the whole; though it may lead to a sterile but ecstatic content, or even to the asylum. In practice, I find, it doesn't—or hasn't yet—make me inefficient. (I am addressing an Adult School on Sunday. I have started a group for studying the Minority Report here. I am going to Cambridge in a week to oversee, with the light of pure reason, the powerful energies of those who are setting forth the new Fabian Rooms,—and later, to put the rising generation, Fabian and otherwise, on the way of Light, all next term.)

"The remedy is Mysticism, or Life, I'm not sure which. Do not leap or turn pale at the word Mysticism, I do not mean any religious thing, or any form of belief. I still burn and torture Christians daily. It is merely the *feeling*—or a kindred one—which underlay the mysticism of the wicked mystics, only I refuse to be cheated by the *feeling* into any kind of *belief*. They were convinced by it that the world was very good, or that the Universe was one, or that God existed. I don't any the more believe the world

to be good. Only I do get rid of the despair
that it isn't—and I certainly seem to see addi-
tional possibilities of its getting better.

"It consists in just looking at people and
things as themselves—neither as useful nor moral
nor ugly nor anything else; but just as being.
At least, that's a philosophical description of it.
What happens is that I suddenly feel the extraordinary value and importance of everybody I
meet, and almost everything I see. In *things*
I am moved in this way especially by some
things; but in people by almost all people. That
is, when the mood is on me. I roam about places
—yesterday I did it even in Birmingham!—and
sit in trains and see the essential glory and
beauty of all the people I meet. I can watch a
dirty middle-aged tradesman in a railway-car-
riage for hours, and love every dirty greasy sulky
wrinkle in his weak chin and every button on his
spotted unclean waistcoat. I know their states
of mind are bad. But I'm so much occupied with
their being there at all, that I don't have time to
think of that. I tell you that a Birmingham
gouty Tariff Reform fifth-rate business man is
splendid and immortal and desirable.

"It's the same about the things of ordinary life.
Half an hour's roaming about a street or village or railway-station shows so much beauty

that it's impossible to be anything but wild with suppressed exhilaration. And it's not only beauty and beautiful things. In a flicker of sunlight on a blank wall, or a reach of muddy pavement, or smoke from an engine at night, there's a sudden significance and importance and inspiration that makes the breath stop with a gulp of certainty and happiness. It's not that the wall or the smoke seem important for anything, or suddenly reveal any general statement, or are rationally seen to be good or beautiful in themselves,—only that *for you* they're perfect and unique. It's like being in love with a person. One doesn't (nowadays, and if one's clean-minded) think the person better or more beautiful or larger than the truth. Only one is extraordinarily excited that the person, exactly as he is, uniquely and splendidly just exists. It's a feeling, not a belief. Only it's a feeling that has amazing results. I suppose my occupation is being in love with the universe—or (for it's an important difference), with certain spots and moments and points of it.

"I wish to God I could express myself. I have a vague notion that this is all very incoherent. But the upshot of it is that one's too happy to *feel* pessimistic; and too much impressed by the immense value and potentialities of everything to *believe* in pessimism—for the following reason, and in the following sense. Every action, one knows (as a good Determinist), has an eternal effect. And every action, therefore, which leads on the whole to good, is *'frightfully'* important. For the good mystic knows how jolly 'good' is. It is not a question of either getting to Utopia in the year 2000, or not. There'll be so much good then, and so much evil. And we can affect it. There—from the purely rational point of view—is the beginning and end of the whole matter. It oughtn't to make any difference to our efforts whether the good in 2000 A.D. will be a lot greater than it is now, or a little greater, or less. In any case, the amount of good we can cause by doing something, or can subtract by not doing it, remains about the same. And that is all that ought to matter.

"Lately, when I've been reading up the Elizabethans, and one or two other periods, I've been amazed more than ever at the way things change. Even in talking to my uncle of seventy about the Victorians, it comes out astoundingly. The whole machinery of life, and the minds of every class and kind of man, change beyond recognition every generation. I don't know that 'Progress' is certain. All I know is that change is. These solid solemn provincials, and old maids,

and business men, and all the immovable system
of things I see round me, will vanish like smoke.
All this present overwhelming reality will be
as dead and odd and fantastic as crinolines, or
'a dish of tay.' Something will be in its place,
inevitably. And what that something will be,
depends on me. With such superb work to do,
and with the wild adventure of it all, and with
the other minutes (too many of them) given to
the enchantment of being even for a moment
alive in a world of real matter (not that imitation, gilt, stuff one gets in Heaven) and actual
people,—I have no time now to be a pessimist.

"I don't know why I have scribbled down
these thin insane vapourings. I don't suppose
you're still as desperate as you were when you
wrote in June. When are you coming to Cambridge? I am going to Germany for the spring
term. But if you can get there next term, are
you coming out to stay at Grantchester? I lead
a lovely and dim and rustic life there, and have
divine food. Hugh is going to be in London,
and —— is old as the hills and withered as a'
spider, and I am the oldest Fabian left (except
——, who is senile), and I dodder about and
smile with toothless gums on all the gay young
sparks of the Fabian Society, to whom I am
more than a father.

"So you might tell me if you are going to shake off for a day or a month the ghastly coils of British Family Life and of Modern Industry that you are wound in, and come to see the bovine existence of a farmer.

"In the name of God and the Republic,

RUPERT."

The next event was a journey on the Continent at the beginning of 1911. He conceived romantic plans for it, as appears in the latter part of this letter to Geoffrey Fry, written before he started, to thank for a present of Mr. Bullen's Elizabethan Songbooks: "I read them when I ought to be learning German, and I writhe with vain passion and with envy. How did they do it? Was it, as we're told, because they always wrote to tunes? The lightness! There are moments when I try to write 'songs', 'where Lumpkin with his Giles hobnobs', but they are bumping rustic guffaws. I feel that sense of envious incompetence and a vast angry clumsiness that hippopotamuses at the Zoo must feel when you stand before them with your clouded cane and take snuff. They're occasionally—the songbooks, not the hippopotamuses—so like the Anthology, and oh! I can see why Headlam loved them.

"I may see you yet in England. For I don't go till January 8 or so. But when I do go, aha! England will never see me more. I shall grow my red whiskers and take to Art. In a few years you may come and stay with me in my villa at Sybaris, or my palace near Smyrna, or my tent at Kandahar, or my yacht off the Cyclades. But you will be a respectable lawyer. You will waggle your pince-nez and lecture me on my harem. Then a large one-eyed negro Eunuch will come and tie you up and pitch you into the sea. And I shall continue to paint sea-scapes in scarlet and umber."

These dreams were not realised. He began his travels with three months in Munich, where he wrote to Mrs. Cornford in the middle of February: "The worst of solitude—or the best—is, that one begins poking at his own soul, examining it, cutting the soft and rotten parts away. And where's one to stop? Have you ever had, at lunch or dinner, an over-ripe pear or apple, and, determined to make the best of it, gone on slicing off the squashy bits? You may imagine me, in München, at a German lunch with Life, discussing hard, and cutting away at the bad parts of the dessert. 'Oh!' says Life, courteous as ever, 'I'm sure you've got a bad soul there. Please don't go on with it! Leave it, and take another! I'm so sorry!' But, knowing I've taken the last, and polite anyhow, 'Oh, no, *please!*' I say, scraping away. 'It's really all right. It's only a little gone, here and there, on the outside. There's plenty that's quite good. I'm quite enjoying it. You always have such delightful souls!' . . . And after a minute, when there's a circle of messy brown rounding my plate, and in the centre a rather woe-begone brown-white thin shapeless scrap, the centre of the thing, Life breaks in again, seeing my plight. —'Oh, but you can't touch any of that! It's bad right through! I'm sure Something must have got in to it! Let me ring for another! There's sure to be some in the larder.' . . . But it won't do, you know. So I rather ruefully reply, 'Ye-es, I'm afraid it *is* impossible. But I won't have another, thanks. I don't really want one at all. I only took it out of mere greed, and to have something to do. Thank you, I've had quite enough—such excellent meat and pudding! I've done splendidly—BUT TO GO ON WITH OUR CONVERSATION ABOUT LITERATURE,—YOU WERE SAYING, I THINK . . .?' and so the incident's at an end.

"Dear! dear! it's very trying being so exalted one day and ever so desperate the next—this Self-knowledge (*why* did that old fool class it

with Self-reverence and Self-control? They're
rarely seen together!) But so one lives in
Munich.

"—And then your letter came! So many
thanks. It made me shake with joy to know that
Cambridge and England (as I know it) was all
as fine as ever. That Jacques and Ka should
be sitting in a café, looking just like themselves
—oh God! what an incredibly lovely superb
world. I fairly howled my triumph down the
ways of this splendid city. 'Oh! you fat, muddy-
faced, grey, jolly Germans who despise me because I don't know your rotten language! Oh!
the people I know, and you don't! Oh! you poor
things!' And they all growl at me because they
don't know why I glory over them. But, of
course, part of the splendour is that—if they
only knew it—they too, these Germans, are all
sitting in cafés and looking just like themselves.
That knowledge sets me often dreaming in a
vague, clerical, world-misty spirit over my solitary coffee, in one of the innumerable cafés here
in which I spend my days. I find myself smiling
a dim, gentle, poetic, paternal, Jehovah-like
smile—over the ultimate excellence of humanity
—at people of, obviously, the most frightful lives
and reputations at other tables; who come pres-
ently sidling towards me. My mysticism van-

ishes, and in immense terror I fly suddenly into the street.

"Oh, but they're a kindly people. Every night I sit in a café near here, after the opera, and read the day-old *Times* (!) and drink—prepare to hear the depths of debauchery into which the young are led in these wicked foreign cities!— HOT MILK, a large glassful. Last night I spilt the whole of the hot milk over myself, while I was trying to negotiate the Literary Supplement. You've no idea how much of one a large glass of hot milk will cover. I was entirely white, except for my scarlet face. All the people in the café crowded round and dabbed me with dirty pocket-handkerchiefs. A kindly people. Nor did I give in. I ordered more hot milk and finished my Supplement, damp but International.

"No! Cambridge isn't very dim and distant, nor Dent a pink shade. I somehow manage, these days, to be aware of two places at once. I used to find it wasn't worth while; and to think that the great thing was to let go completely of a thing when you've done with it, and turn wholly and freshly to the next. 'Being able to take and to let go and to take, and knowing when to take and when to let go, and knowing that life's this— is the only way to happiness' is the burden of the

Marschallin in the *Rosencavalier* (the rage of
Germany just now). There's some truth in it.
But sometimes, now, I find I can weave two ex-
istences together and enjoy both, and be aware
of the unique things of each. It's true that as
I write there's an attitude of Jacques's, or a slow
laugh of Ka's, or a moon at Grantchester, or a
speech of Dickinson's, that I'd love, and that I'm
missing. But there'll be other such, no doubt, in
May and June—and what if I'd not met the
lovable Mr. Leuba (and so differently lovable
from an English unsuccessful journalist!) or the
fascinating Miss Something or Other of Paris,
or the interesting and wicked di Ravelli, or Dr.
Wolfskell who is shy and repeats Swinburne in
large quantities with a villainous German accent
but otherwise knows no English, or that bearded
man in the café, or the great Hegedus, or Professor Sametscu? . . .

"Eh, but I have grown clerical and solemn and
moral. That is because I've been seeing so much
Ibsen lately. I apologise. I'm old-fashioned
enough to admire that man vastly. I've seen five
or six of his plays in four weeks. They always
leave me prostrate.

"No, I've not yet been proposed to by young
ladies in plaid blouses, not even one at a time.
As a matter of fact I know only one or two

such. Most of the people I see are working at some sensible thing like writing, music, or painting, and are free and comradely. I made one or two incursions into Anglo-German Philistia, and came hurriedly forth. I'm damnably sorry for the plaid blouses (who *do* exist there, and are, at present, so much better than their mothers). I saw two stifling and crying. But I'm not going back to rescue them.

"But in ordinary, and nicer, ways, I meet a lot of jolly people. It's true, a lot, I think, what you say about friends; but oh, dear people! it *is* fun going away and making thousands of acquaintances.

"I finish this tourist's effusion at 2 o' the morning, sitting up in bed, with my army blanket round me. My feet, infinitely disconnected, and southward, inform me that to-night it is freezing again. The bed is covered with Elizabethan and German books I may or may not read ere I sleep. In the distance glimmers the gaunt white menacing Ibsenite stove that casts a gloom over my life. The Algerian dancing-master next door is, for once, quiet. I rather think the Dragon overhead (the Dragon = that monstrous, tired-faced, screeching, pouchy creature, of infinite age and horror, who screams opposite me at dinner and talks with great crags of food projecting from her mouth; a decayed Countess, they say) is snoring.

"Oh, I sometimes make a picture of Conduit Head, with Jacques in a corner, and Gwen on other cushions, and Justin on his back, and Ka on a footstool, and Francis smoking, and Frances in the chair to the right (facing the fire). . . . It stands out against the marble of the Luitpold Café and then fades. . . . But say it's true!

"Even with an enormous stomach and a beard and in Munich.—Yours, RUPERT."

From Munich he went to join his godfather, Mr. Robert Whitelaw, in Florence, where he wrote to me at the end of April: "I led a most noisome life in Munich, crawling about in trams, and eating, and sleeping. I never thought, and barely ever read. I worked hard in an intermittent doleful way, but never accomplished anything. I spent two months over a poem that describes the feelings of a fish, in the metre of *L'Allegro*. It was meant to be a lyric, but has turned into a work of 76 lines with a moral end. It's quite unintelligible. Beyond that I have written one or two severe and subtle sonnets in my most modern manner—descriptions of very poignant and complicated situations in the life of to-day, thrilling with a false simplicity. The one beginning

'I did not think you thought I knew you knew'

has created a sensation in English-speaking circles in Munich.

"I have sampled and sought out German culture. It has changed all my political views. I am wildly in favour of nineteen new Dreadnoughts. German culture must never, never prevail! The Germans are nice, and well-meaning, and they try; but they are SOFT. Oh! they *are* soft! The only good things (outside music perhaps) are the writings of Jews who live in Vienna. Have you ever heard of Mr. Schnitzler's historical play? They act an abbreviated version which lasts from 7 to 12. I saw it. A Hebrew journalist's version of the *Dynasts,* but rather good.

"Here I live in a *pension* surrounded by English clergymen and ladies. They are all Forster characters. Perhaps it is his pension.[1] But to live among Forster characters is too bewildering. The 'quaint' remarks fall all round one during meal-times, with little soft plups like pats of butter. 'So strong,' they said, next to me, at the concert last night, of the Fifth Symphony; 'and

[1] See E. M. Forster's "A Room with a View."

yet so restful, my dear! not at all what I should call *morbid,* you know!' Just now the young parson and his wife, married a fortnight, have been conversing. 'Are you ready to kick off?' he said. How extraordinary! What does it mean? I *gathered* it merely meant was she dressed for San Lorenzo. But does the Church talk like that nowadays?

"So I am seeing life. But I am thirsting for Grantchester. I am no longer to be at *The Orchard,* but next door at *The Old Vicarage,* with a wonderful garden. I shall fly from Florence, which is full of painstaking ugly pictures. But before I go I've got to settle the question, 'Shall I lay a handful of roses on Mrs. Browning's grave? and, if so, how many?' These literary problems are dreadful. And the English Cemetery is so near!"

"It's very late," he wrote one evening to the Raverats. "The stars over Fiesole are wonderful; and there are quiet cypresses and a straight white wall opposite. I renounce England; though at present I've the senile affection of a godfather for it. I think of it, over there (beyond even Fiesole)—Gwen and Jacques and Ka and Frances and Justin and Dudley, and Dr. Verrall and the Master, and Lord Esher and Mr. Balfour. Good-night, children."

IV

The Old Vicarage, which was his home in 1911, is a long, low, ramshackle, tumble-down one-storied house, with attics in a high roof, and a verandah. It has a profuse, overgrown, sweet-smelling, 'most individual and bewildering' garden, with random trees and long grass, and here and there odd relics of the eighteenth century, a sundial sticking out from the dried-up basin of a round pond, and an imitation ruin in a corner. Towards the end of the year it is a little melancholy. "The garden," he wrote in September, "is immeasurably autumnal, sad, mysterious, august. I walk in it feeling like a fly crawling on the score of the Fifth Symphony"; and in December he called it a House of Usher. But in summer it's a paradise of scent and colour. "You'll find me quite wild with reading and the country," he wrote in an invitation. "Come prepared for bathing, and clad in primitive clothes. Bring books also: one talks eight hours, reads eight, and sleeps eight."

Here is a morning of about this time, in a letter to Miss Katherine Cox: "I worked till 1, and then ran nearly to Haslingfield and back before lunch, thinking over the next bits. There was such clearness and frosty sun. Some men under a haystack, eating their lunch, shouted how fine a day it was. I shouted back it was very cold; and ran on. They roared with laughter and shouted after me that with that fine crop of hair I oughtn't to be cold. . . . It was wonderful and very clean out there. I thought of all you Londoners, dirty old drivellers! Now I'm come in to rehearse my nigger part [as a super in the *Magic Flute*] and to work. I've realised that taking part in theatrical performances is the only thing worth doing. And it's so *very* nice being an intelligent subordinate. I'm a very good subordinate—it's such a test. I'm thought not to dance well: but my intelligence and devotion have brought me rapidly to the front. I am now the most important of 7 negroes!"

He was now working at the first draft of his dissertation on John Webster, which he sent in at the end of the year. "I've wallowed in Webster-Texts all day," he wrote in September. "If only I didn't want, at the same time, to be reading everything else in the world, I should be infinitely happy." He didn't get the Fellowship till next year.

He was also preparing the book of *Poems* which Messrs. Sidgwick & Jackson published in December. It had a mixed reception, both from

his friends and from the critics. I was lucky
enough to take it in a way which pleased him;
and he rewarded me with the following letter,
which is too informing to be left out, though I
would rather it fell to someone else to print it:
"Your letter gave me great joy. I horribly feel
that degrading ecstasy that I have always de-
spised in parents whose shapeless offspring are
praised for beauty. People are queer about my
poems. Some that I know very well and have
great *sympathie* with, don't like them. Some
people seem to like them. Some like only the
early ones—them considerably, but the others
not at all. Th ̥e rather sadden me. I hobnob
vaguely with them over the promising verses of
a young poet, called Rupert Brooke, who died
in 1908. But I'm so much more concerned
with the living, who doesn't interest them.
God! it's so cheering to find someone who likes
the modern stuff, and appreciates what one's at.
You can't think how your remarks and liking
thrilled me. You seemed, both in your classing
them and when you got to details, to agree so
closely with what I felt about them (only, of
course, I often feel doubtful about their rela-
tive value to other poetry) that I knew you
understood what they meant. It sounds a poor
compliment—or else a queer conceitedness—to

remark on your understanding them; but it's really been rather a shock to me—and made me momentarily hopeless—that so many intelligent and well-tasted people didn't seem to have any idea what I was driving at, in any poem of the last few years. It opened my eyes to the fact that people who like poetry are barely more common than people who like pictures.

"I'm (of course) unrepentant about the 'unpleasant' poems.[1] I don't claim great merit for the *Channel Passage:* but the point of it was (or should have been!) 'serious.' There are common and sordid things—situations or details— that may suddenly bring all tragedy, or at least the brutality of actual emotions, to you. I rather grasp relievedly at them, after I've beaten vain hands in the rosy mists of poets' experiences. Lear's button, and Hilda Lessways turning the gas suddenly on, and—but you know more of them than I. Shakespeare's not unsympathetic. 'My mistress' eyes are nothing like the sun.' And the emotions of a sea-sick lover seem to me at least as poignant as those of the hero who has 'brain-fever.' . . . . . .

"Mrs. Cornford tried to engage me in a controversy over the book—she and her school. They

---

[1] I had expressed an apologetic preference for poems that I could read at meals.

are known as the Heart-criers, because they believe all poetry ought to be short, simple, naïve,
and a cry from the heart; the sort of thing an
inspired only child might utter if it was in the
habit of posing to its elders. They object to
my poetry as unreal, affected, complex, 'literary,'
and full of long words. I'm re-writing English
literature on their lines. Do you think this is
a fair rendering of Shakespeare's first twenty
sonnets, if Mrs. Cornford had had the doing of
them?

TRIOLET

If you would only have a son,
   William, the day would be a glad one.
It *would* be nice for everyone,
If you would only have a son.
And, William, what would *you* have done
   If Lady Pembroke hadn't had one?
If you would only have a son,
   William, the day *would* be a glad one!

It seems to me to have got the kernel of the situation, and stripped away all unnecessary verbiage
or conscious adornment."

The verdicts of the newspapers varied from
that of the *Saturday Review,* which "definitely
told Mr. Rupert Brooke to 'mar no more trees
with writing love-songs in their barks,'" to that

of the *Daily Chronicle,* which prophesied, by the
mouth of Edward Thomas, that he would be a
poet, and not a little one. It may be said that in
general the book was received with a good deal
of interest, and hailed as at least promising.
Many of the critics seemed so struck with the
'unpleasant' poems (seven, at most, out of fifty)
that they could hardly notice the others. This
showed, perhaps, a wrong sense of proportion;
but the author's own point of view about them
is certainly a matter of interest, and though the
purpose of this memoir is not critical, it may be
worth while here to put together some of its
factors, besides those which appear from the letter I have just quoted. It is, of course, absurdly
untrue that, as has been said, he felt he ought to
make up for his personal beauty by being ugly
in his poetry. To begin with, ugliness had a
quite unaffected attraction for him; he thought
it just as *interesting* as anything else; he didn't
like it—he loathed it—but he liked thinking about
it. 'The poetical character,' as Keats said, 'lives
in gusto.' Then he still had at this age (24) a
good deal of what soon afterwards faded completely away—the bravado, the feeling that it
was fun to shock and astonish the respectable,
which came out in his school letters. Again, he
was incensed by the usual attitude of criticism—

in his view, either stupid or hypocritical—towards 'coarseness' in literature. "Indeed," he wrote early this year in a review, "the Elizabethans *were* refined. Their stories were shocking, their thoughts nasty, their language indelicate. It is absurd to want them otherwise. It is intolerable that these critics should shake the pedagogic finger of amazed reproval at them. . . . . . . Such people do not understand that the vitality of the Elizabethan Drama is inseparable from [its coarseness]. Their wail that its realism is mingled with indecency is more than once repeated. True literary realism, they think, is a fearless reproduction of what real living men say when there is a clergyman in the room." The feeling here expressed urged him to make a demonstration; it dignified the boyish impulse into a duty.

To conclude this subject I will quote a letter to his publisher about the sonnet *Libido*, to which the original title *Lust* is now restored: "My own feeling is that to remove it would be to overbalance the book still more in the direction of unimportant prettiness. There's plenty of that sort of wash in the other pages for the readers who like it. They needn't read the parts which are new and serious. About a lot of the book I occasionally feel that like Ophelia I've turned 'thought and affliction, passion, hell itself, to favour and to prettiness.' So I'm extra keen about the places where I think that thought and passion are, however clumsily, *not* so transmuted. This was one of them. It seemed to have qualities of reality and novelty that made up for the clumsiness. . . . I should like it to stand, as a representative in the book of abortive poetry against literary verse; and because I can't see any æsthetic ground against it which would not damn three-quarters of the rest of the book too; or any moral ground at all."

During all this time he was working up to a rather serious illness. As a child and as a boy he had been delicate, but at Cambridge his health had greatly improved, and all the time he was there he never had to go to a doctor. Now, however, he left his open-air life and came to London for work on Webster. "He lived," his Mother tells me, "in wretched rooms in Charlotte Street, spending all day at the British Museum, going round to his friends in the evening and sitting up most of the night. He then went to Grantchester to finish his dissertation, and from his brother's account scarcely went to bed at all for a week, several times working all night. He came home for Christmas quite tired out." The letter to me which I last quoted, written at Rugby on the 22nd of December, ends with this: "I'm sorry I never saw you again. The last part of November and the first of December I spent in writing my dissertation at Grantchester. . . . . . . I couldn't do it at all well. I came to London in a dilapidated condition for a day or two after it was over. Now I'm here over Christmas. About the 27th I go to Lulworth with a reading-party for a fortnight. Then to the South of France, then Germany . . . and the future's mere mist. I want to stay out of England for some time. (1) I don't like it. (2) I want to work—a play, and so on. (8) I'm rather tired and dejected.

"So I *probably* shan't be in London for some time. If I am, I'll let you know. I'm going to try to do scraps—reviewing, etc.—in my spare time for the immediate future. I suppose you don't edit a magazine? I might review Elizabethan books at some length for the *Admiralty Gazette* or *T.A.T.* (Tattle amongst Tars), or whatever journal you officially produce? At least I hope you'll issue an order to include my poems in the library of all submarines."

His next letter is of February 25th, 1912, from Rugby: "I went to Lulworth after Christmas for a reading party. There I collapsed sud-

denly into a foodless and sleepless Hell. God!
how one can suffer from what my amiable spe-
cialist described as a 'nervous breakdown.' (He
reported that I had got into a 'seriously intro-
spective condition'! and—more tangibly—that
my weight had gone down a stone or two.)   I
tottered, being too tired for suicide, to Cannes,
not because I like the b—— place, but because
my mother happened to be there.   I flapped
slowly towards the surface there; and rose a little more at Munich.   I have come here for a
month or two to complete it.   After that I shall
be allowed (and, by Phœbus, able, I hope) to
do some work.   My cure consists in perpetual
over-eating and over-sleeping, no exercise, and
no thought.   Rather a nice existence, but oh
God! weary."

In March he went for a walk in Sussex with
James Strachey, and sent Miss Cox a sensational
account, dated from 'The Mermaid Club, Rye,'
of an unsuccessful attempt to visit a great man
whose acquaintance he had made at Cambridge.
"I read the 'Way of All Flesh' and talk to
James.   James and I have been out this evening
to call on Mr. Henry James at 9.0.   We found—
at length—the house.   It was immensely rich,
and brilliantly lighted at every window on the

ground floor. The upper floors were deserted: one black window open. The house is straight on the street. We nearly fainted with fear of a company. At length I pressed the Bell of the Great Door—there was a smaller door further along, the servants' door we were told. No answer. I pressed again. At length a slow dragging step was heard within. It stopped inside the door. We shuffled. Then, very slowly, very loudly, immense numbers of chains and bolts were drawn within. There was a pause again. Further rattling within. Then the steps seemed to be heard retreating. There was silence. We waited in a wild agonising stupefaction. The house was dead silent. At length there was a shuffling noise from the servants' door. We thought someone was about to emerge from there to greet us. We slid down towards it—nothing happened. We drew back and observed the house. A low whistle came from it. Then nothing for two minutes. Suddenly a shadow passed quickly across the light in the window nearest the door. Again nothing happened. James and I, sick with surmise, stole down the street. We thought we heard another whistle, as we departed. We came back here shaking—we didn't know at what.

"If the evening paper, as you get this, tells of

the murder of Mr. Henry James—you'll know."

By this time he was quite well again. He went to Germany in April, and stayed there for two or three months, mostly with Dudley Ward in Berlin, where he wrote *The Old Vicarage, Grantchester*[1] ("this hurried stuff," he called it when he sent it me). "I read Elizabethans for 2-3 hours a day, quite happily," he wrote to his Mother. "Other work I haven't tried much. I started a short play, and worked at it for two or three hours. I paid the penalty by not getting to sleep till 5 next morning." The play was a one-act melodrama called *Lithuania*, founded on the well-known anecdote of a son coming back with a fortune, after years of absence in America, to his peasant-family, who kill him for his money and then find out who he was. (It was acted in the spring of 1916 by Miss Lillah M'Carthy, Miss Clare Greet, Leon M. Lion, John Drinkwater, and others, at a charity matinée at His Majesty's, together with Gordon Bottomley's *King Lear's Wife* and Wilfrid Gibson's *Hoops;* and was thought to show much promise of dramatic power.)

He came home from Germany as well as ever, to spend the rest of the summer at Grantchester.

---

[1] This poem was first published in the King's magazine *Basileon.* The MS. is now in the Fitzwilliam Museum.

I must here touch upon a change in his outlook, a development of his character, which, as I think, took form during this year from the germs which may be seen in his earlier letters, already quoted, to Mr. Cotterill and to Ben Keeling. Perhaps it was the result of the 'introspection' which contributed to his illness, and to which his illness in its turn gave opportunity. To put it briefly and bluntly, he had discovered that goodness was the most important thing in life—'that immortal beauty and goodness,' as he wrote much later, 'that radiance, to love which is to feel one has safely hold of eternal things.' Since he grew up he had never held (and did n t now acquire) any definite, still less any ready-made, form of religious belief; his ideals had been mainly intellectual; and if he had been asked to define goodness, he would probably have said that it meant having true opinions about ethics. Now he found that it was even more a matter of the heart and of the will; and he did not shrink from avowing his changed view to his old comrades in the life of the mind, some of whom perhaps found it a little disconcerting, a little ridiculous.

Henceforward the only thing that he cared for —or rather felt he ought to care for—in a man, was the possession of goodness; its absence, the one thing that he hated, sometimes with fierceness. He never codified his morals, never made laws for the conduct of others, or for his own; it was the spirit, the passion, that counted with him. "That is the final rule of life, the best one ever made," he wrote next year from the Pacific,— "'Whoso shall offend one of these little ones'— remembering that all the eight hundred millions on earth, except oneself, are the little ones."

In the autumn of this year he began coming to London oftener and for longer visits, usually staying at my rooms in Gray's Inn; going to plays and music halls, seeing pictures, and making numbers of new acquaintances and friends. Henry James, W. B. Yeats and John Masefield he knew already; and he made friends about this time with Edmund Gosse, Walter de la Mare, Wilfrid Gibson, John Drinkwater, W. H. Davies, and many others.

There was a general feeling among the younger poets that modern English poetry was very good, and sadly neglected by readers. Rupert announced one evening, sitting half-undressed on his bed, that he had conceived a brilliant scheme. He would write a book of poetry, and publish it as a selection from the works of twelve different writers, six men and six women, all with the most convincing pseudonyms. That, he thought, *must* make them sit up. It occurred to me that as we both believed there were at least twelve flesh-and-blood poets whose work, if properly thrust under the public's nose, had a good chance of producing the effect he desired, it would be simpler to use the material which was ready to hand. Next day (September 20th it was) we lunched in my rooms with Gibson and Drinkwater, and Harold Monro and Arundel del Re (editor and sub-editor of the then *Poetry Review,* since re-named *Poetry and Drama*), and started the plan of the book which was published in December under the name of *Georgian Poetry, 1911-1912.*

This was our great excitement for the rest of the year. Rupert went to stay with Ward in Berlin for November, and kept sending suggestions for promoting the sale of the book. (Years before, a cynical young friend of ours at King's had told me that though 'Rupert's public form was the youthful poet, the real foundation of his character was a hard business faculty.') "I forget all my other ideas," he wrote, after making some very practical proposals, "but they each sold some 25 copies. I have a hazy vision of incredible *réclame.* You ought to have an immense map of England (*vide* 'Tono-Bungay') and plan campaigns with its aid. And literary charts, each district mapped out, and a fortress secured. John Buchan to fill a page of the *Spectator:* Filson Young in the *P.M.G.* (we shall be seventeen *Things that Matter* in italics?), etc., etc. You'll be able to found a hostel for poor Georgians on the profits." Some of his ideas were too vast, but others were acted on; and though delays of printing and binding kept the book back till a few days before Christmas, frustrating our calculation on huge sales to present-givers, its success outran our wildest hopes.

He spent most of the spring of 1913 in London, enjoying himself in many directions. He went again and again to the Russian Ballet, which he loved ("They, if anything can, redeem our civilisation," he had written in December. "I'd give everything to be a ballet-designer"); and he conceived a passion for the Hippodrome Revue, *Hullo, Ragtime!* which he saw ten times. He had always been on occasion a great fitter-in of things and people, and vast networks of his minute arrangements survive on postcards, though without the finishing strands put in by telephone. He got to know more and more people, including the Asquith family and George Wyndham, with whom he spent a Sunday at Clouds. He had no ambition for the career of a 'young man about town'; but he felt he might let himself go for the moment, as he would be starting for America before he could get too much involved.

He got his Fellowship on March 8th. "It's very good of you to congratulate me," he wrote to Geoffrey Fry. "You can't think how I despise you mere civilians, now. *Jetzt bin ich Professor.* A grey look of learning has already settled on my face. And I wear spectacles." Next week he went to King's to be admitted, or, as he called it, 'churched.' "I dined solemnly," he told Mrs. Cornford, "with very old white-haired men, at one end of a vast dimly-lit hall, and afterwards drank port somnolently in the Common Room, with the College silver, and 17th Century portraits, and a 16th Century fireplace, and 15th Century ideas. The perfect Don, I . . . ."

The only other break in the London life was a visit to Rugby towards the end of March, when he wrote a rapturous spring-letter to Miss Cathleen Nesbitt. "But oh! but oh! such a day! 'Spring came complete with a leap in a day,' said the wisest and nicest man in Warwickshire—my godfather,[1] an aged scholar, infinitely learned in Greek, Latin, English, and Life. He said it was a quotation from Browning. It certainly

[1] Mr. Whitelaw.

fitted. I took him a walk. The air had changed all in a night, and had that soft caressingness, and yet made you want to jump and gambol. *Alacer*, and not *acer*, was, we agreed, the epithet for the air. Oh! it's mad to be in London with the world like this. I can't tell you of it. The excitement and music of the birds, the delicious madness of the air, the blue haze in the distance, the straining of the hedges, the green mist of shoots about the trees—oh, it wasn't in these details—it was beyond and round them—something that included them. It's the sort of day that brought back to me what I've had so rarely for the last two years—that tearing hunger to do and do and do things. I want to walk 1000 miles, and write 1000 plays, and sing 1000 poems, and drink 1000 pots of beer, and kiss 1000 girls, and —oh, a million things! . . . . . . The spring makes me almost ill with excitement. I go round corners on the roads shivering and nearly crying with suspense, as one did as a child, fearing some playmate in waiting to jump out and frighten one."

V

On May 22nd he started for New York on a year's travels. "You won't see me again till I'm a bold, bad, bearded broncho-buster in a red shirt and riding-breeches," he wrote to Miss Sybil Pye. His plans were vague, and at that time he expected to be back by the end of 1913. He had written to his mother in February, to explain: "I think, now my physical health is quite all right, I shall go off to America or somewhere. I feel just as I did in the autumn, that it's no good going on in England. . . . . . . It is only wasting time to go on without doing proper work. I think of going off to California or somewhere, and doing some kind of work, or tramping. I shall take what money I have, and if they don't give me a fellowship, I can capitalise £200 or so, and that'll last me for as long as I want to be abroad. I have no fear about being able to make a living now, for there are so many papers that'll print anything by me whenever I like."

"We may meet again in this world," he wrote to the Raverats, "I brown and bearded, you mere red round farmers. When that'll be, I know not. Perhaps in six months. Perhaps in six years. Or we may only find each other in a whiter world, nighty-clad, harped, winged, celibate.

Shall we go walks along the hills of Heaven,
Rücksack on back and aureole in pocket,
And stay in Paradisal pubs, and drink

> Immortal toasts in old ambrosia,
> Fry wings in nectar on the glassy sea,
> And build the fire with twigs of amaranth?"

Here is his farewell to England, in a letter to a friend from the s.s. *Cedric:* "I arrived solitary on the boat. After it started I went to the office, more to show that I existed than in the dimmest hope of getting anything—and there was stuck up a list called 'Unclaimed Mail.' (I thought it sounded as if a lot of the Knights who had promised to equip themselves for the Quest of the Holy Grail had missed the train, or married a wife, or overslept, or something.) And at the top of the list 'Mr. Rupert Brooke.' . . . . . .

"—day. Time is no more. I have been a million years on this boat. I don't know if it's this month or last or next. Sometimes, remotely, in a past existence, I was on land. But this is another existence. . . . I have my joys. Today I ate *clam-chowder*. That's romance, isn't it? I ordered it quite recklessly. I didn't know what it was. I only knew that anything called *clam-chowder* must be strange beyond words.

> If you were like clam-chowder
> And I were like the spoon,
> And the band were playing louder
> And a little more in tune,

I'd stir you till I spilled you,
Or kiss you till I killed you,
If you were like clam-chowder
And I were like the spoon.

(But you don't know Swinburne.) 'Clam-chowder,' my God! what am I coming to? . . .

"I haven't told you much about my voyage, have I? There's not much to tell. I felt, before I got your letter, a trifle lonely at Liverpool. Everybody else seemed to have people to see them off. So I went back on shore and found a dirty little boy, who was unoccupied, and said his name was William. 'Will you wave to me if I give you sixpence, William?' I said. 'Why yes,' said William. So I gave him sixpence, and went back on board. And when the time came he leaned over his railing on the landing-stage, and waved. And now and then he shouted indistinct messages in a shrill voice. And as we slid away, the last object I looked at was a small dot waving a white handkerchief, or nearly white, faithfully. So I got my sixpenn'orth and my farewell—Dear William!"

For his travels in America and Canada, his letters to the *Westminster Gazette*, since republished, must be allowed in the main to speak; but these may be supplemented by scraps of his letters to his mother and his friends. "America hasn't changed me much yet," he wrote from New York. "I've got the adorablest little touch of an American accent, and I'm a bit thinner." He wasn't very happy at first. "When I'm alone," he wrote to me on June 29th from the Montreal Express, "I sink into a kind of mental stupor which may last for months. I shan't be really right till I get back to you all." And again from Ottawa, ten days later, "I don't get very miserable, or go to pieces (save for occasional bursts of home-sickness just before meals); but my whole level of life descends to an incredible muddy flatness. I do no reading, no thinking, no writing. And very often I don't see many things. The real hell of it is that I get so numb that my brain and senses don't record fine or clear impressions. So the time is nearly all waste. I'm very much ashamed of it all. For I've always beforehand a picture of myself dancing through foreign cities, drinking in novelty, hurling off letters to the *W.G.*, breaking into song and sonnet, dashing off plays and novels. . . . Lord, Lord! . . . . . .

"American 'hospitality' means that with the nice ones you can be at once on happy and intimate terms. Oh dear, the tears quite literally well up into my eyes when I think of a group of young Harvard people I tumbled into—at Harvard. They had the charm and freshness and capacity for instantly creating a relation of happy and warm friendliness that, for instance, Denis [1] has. It's a nice thing . . . . . .

"You, at home, have no conception how you're all getting a sanctity and halo about you in my mind. I dwell so much and so sentimentally on all the dear dead days that I am beginning to see no faults and all virtues in all of you. *You*, my dear, appear perfection in every part. Your passion for anagrams is a lovable and deeply intellectual taste. Your acquaintance with [a *bête noire* of his] a beautiful thing. Your lack of sympathy with the Labour Party turns to a noble and picturesque Toryism. Even your preference for gilded over comfortable chairs loses something of its ugliness in my heart. Of you and Norton and Duncan and —— and even —— I think incessantly, devotedly, and tearfully. Even of figures who, to be frank, have hovered but dimly on the outskirts of my consciousness, I am continually and fragrantly memorial. . . . . . . I make up little minor, pitiful songs, the burden of which is that I have a folk-longing to get back from all this Imperial luxury to the simplicity of the little places and quiet folks I

[1] Denis Browne, of whom more hereafter.

knew and loved. One very beautiful one has the chorus—

Would God I were eating plover's eggs,
   And drinking dry champagne,
With the Bernard Shaws, Mr. and Mrs. Masefield, Lady
   Horner, Neil Primrose, Raleigh, the Right Honourable
   Augustine Birrell, Eddie, six or seven Asquiths, and
   Felicity Tree,
   In Downing Street again."

His next letter was from Toronto, a fortnight later: "I've found here an Arts and Letters Club of poets, painters, journalists, etc., where they'd heard of me, and read *G. P.*,[1] and, oh Eddie, one fellow actually possessed my 'Poems.' Awful Triumph. Every now and then one comes up and presses my hand and says, 'Wal Sir, you cannot know what a memorable Day in my life this is.' Then I do my pet boyish-modesty stunt and go pink all over; and everyone thinks it *too* delightful. One man said to me, 'Mr. Brooks' (my Canadian name), 'Sir, I may tell you that in my opinion you have Mr. Noyes skinned.' That means I'm better than him: a great compliment. But they're really quite an up-to-date lot; and very cheery and pleasant. I go to-morrow to the desert and the wilds."

[1] *Georgian Poetry.*

The desert and the wilds suited him much better than the cities. "Today," he wrote to Miss Nesbit on the 3rd of August from Lake George, about 70 miles from Winnipeg, "I'm 26 years old—and I've done so little. I'm very much ashamed. By God, I am going to make things hum though—but that's all so far away. I'm lying quite naked on a beach of golden sand, 6 miles away from the hunting-lodge, the other man near by, a gun between us in case bears appear, the boat pulled up on the shore, the lake very blue and ripply, and the sun rather strong. . . . . . . We caught two pike on the way out, which lie picturesquely in the bows of the boat. Along the red-gold beach are the tracks of various wild animals, mostly jumping-deer and caribou. One red-deer we saw as we came round the corner, lolloping along the beach, stopping and snuffling the wind, and then going on again. Very lovely. We were up-wind and it didn't see us, and the meat wasn't needed, so we didn't shoot at it (I'm glad, I'm no 'sportsman'). We bathed off the beach, and then lit a fire of birch and spruce, and fried eggs, and ate cold caribou-heart, and made tea, and had, oh! blueberry pie. Cooking and eating a meal naked is the most solemnly primitive thing one can do; and—this is the one thing which will make you realise that

I'm living far the most wonderfully and incredibly romantic life you ever heard of, and infinitely superior to your miserable crawling London existence—the place we landed at is an INDIAN CAMP. At any moment a flotilla of birchbark canoes may sweep round the corner, crowded with Indians, braves and squaws and papooses— and not those lonely half-breeds and stray Indians that speak English, mind you, but the Real Thing! Shades of Fenimore Cooper!"

But he was quite able to cope with civilisation when he got back to it. The next letter is ten days later, from Edmonton: "I find I'm becoming very thick-skinned and bold, and the complete journalist. I've just been interviewed by a reporter. I fairly crushed him. I just put my cigar in the corner of my mouth, and undid my coat-buttons, and put my thumbs under my armpits, and spat, and said, 'Say, Kid, this is some town.' He asked me a lot of questions to which I didn't know the answers, so I lied. . . . . . .

"Also I am become very good at bearding people. I just enter railway offices and demand free passes as a journalist, and stamp into immense newspaper buildings and say I want to talk for an hour to the Chief Editor, and I can lean across the counter with a cigarette and dis-

cuss the Heart with the young lady who sells
cigars, newspapers, and stamps. I believe I
could do a deal in Real Estate, in the bar, over
a John Collins, with a clean-shaven Yankee with
a tremulous eyelid and a moist lower lip. In
fact, I am a Man."

He stayed some days at Vancouver, where he
wrote his mother a letter which gives me occasion
to stand in a very white sheet. "I'm glad you
like the Westminster articles. They're not
always very well written, but I think they're
the sort of stuff that ought to interest an intelligent *W.G.* reader more than the ordinary travel
stuff one sees. I hope they won't annoy people
over this side. Canadians and Americans are
so touchy. But it's absurd to ladle out indis-
criminate praise, as most people do. I heard
from Eddie about the proofs. I was very sad
at one thing. In my first or second article I had
made an American say 'You bet your'—which is
good American slang. Eddie thought a word
was left out and inserted *'boots.'* I only hope
the *W.G.* omitted it. I suppose it'll be printed
by now. If not, 'phone the *W.G.* or write—
But it must be too late. Alas! Alas!

"Vancouver is a queer place, rather different
from the rest of Canada. More oriental. The
country and harbour are rather beautiful, with

great violet mountains all round, snow-peaks in the distance. They interviewed me and put (as usual) a quite inaccurate report of it in the paper, saying I'd come here to investigate the Japanese question. In consequence about five people rang me up every morning at 8 o'clock (British Columbians get up an hour earlier than I) to say they wanted to wait on me and give me their views. Out here they always have telephones in the bedrooms. One old sea-captain came miles to tell me that the Japanese—and every other—trouble was due to the fact that British Columbia had neglected the teaching of the Gospels on the land question. He wasn't so far out in some respects."

He sailed for Hawaii from San Francisco, where he was warmly welcomed at Berkeley University by Professor Gayly and Professor Wells, and made many friends among the undergraduates. "California," he wrote to me on the 1st of October, "is nice, and the Californians a friendly bunch. There's a sort of goldenness about 'Frisco and the neighbourhood. It hangs in the air, and about the people. Everyone is very cheery and cordial and simple. They are rather a nation apart, different from the rest of the States. Much more like the English. As everywhere in this extraordinary country, I am welcomed with open arms when I say I know Masefield and Goldie![1] It's very queer. I can't for the life of me help moving about like a metropolitan among rustics, or an Athenian in Thrace. Their wide-mouthed awe at England is so touching—they really are a colony of ours still. That they should be speaking to a man who knows Lowes Dickinson, has met Galsworthy, who once saw Belloc plain! . . . What should we feel if we could speak with an *habitué* of the theatre at Athens, Fifth Century, or with Mine Host of the Mermaid? All that they have with me, the dears! Yet I don't know why I write this from California, the one place that has a literature and tradition of its own.

"On Tuesday—the Pacific. I'll write thence, but God knows when it'll get to you."

He wrote no letters to the *Westminster* from the South Seas, chiefly because the life there was too absorbing, but partly perhaps from doubt whether they would be used. He had got a letter from which he inferred, wrongly, that only one series of six letters was wanted from him. "Isn't it beastly?" he wrote. "I supposed I was going on once a week for months and years. I could read me once a week for ever, couldn't you?" But there are plenty of letters to friends.

[1] G. Lowes Dickinson.

"The Pacific," he wrote from the steamer on October 12th, "has been very pacific, God be thanked—so I've had a pleasant voyage. Three passionate Pacific women cast lustrous eyes towards me, but, with a dim remembrance of the fate of Conrad characters who succumbed to such advances, I evade them. I pass my hand wearily through my long hair, and say, 'Is not the soul of Maurya a glimmering wing in the moth-hour?' or words to that effect. The Celtic method is not understood in this part of the world."

The first stop was at Honolulu, where he stayed on Waikiki beach, the scene of the sonnet beginning "Warm perfumes like a breath from vine and tree." He wrote to his mother without enthusiasm: "Honolulu itself is a dreadfully American place, just like any city in the States or Canada"; and he found little better to say of the country round about than that "it really *is* tropical in character, like some of the gardens and places at Cannes, on an immense scale."

But this is what he wrote to me about Samoa from the steamer taking him to Fiji: "It's all true about the South Seas! I get a little tired of it at moments, because I am just too old for Romance. But there it is; there it wonderfully is;

heaven on earth, the ideal life, little work, dancing and singing and eating; naked people of incredible loveliness, perfect manners, and immense kindliness, a divine tropic climate, and intoxicating beauty of scenery. I wandered with an 'interpreter'—entirely genial and quite incapable of English—through Samoan villages. The last few days I stopped in one, where a big marriage feast was going on. I lived in a Samoan house (the coolest in the world) with a man and his wife, nine children ranging from a proud beauty of 18 to a round object of 1 year, a dog, a cat, a proud hysterical hen, and a gaudy scarlet and green parrot who roved the roof and beams with a wicked eye, choosing a place whence to —— twice a day, with humorous precision, on my hat and clothes.

"The Samoan girls have extraordinarily beautiful bodies, and walk like goddesses. They're a lovely brown colour, without any black Melanesian admixture. Can't you imagine how shattered and fragmentary a heart I'm bearing away to Fiji and Tahiti? And, oh dear! I'm afraid they'll be just as bad.

"And it's all true about, for instance, cocoanuts. You tramp through a strange, vast, dripping, tropical forest for hours, listening to weird liquid hootings from birds and demons in the branches above. Then you feel thirsty. So you send your boy up a great perpendicular palm. He runs up with utter ease and grace, cuts off a couple of vast nuts, and comes down and makes holes in them. And they're chock-full of the best drink in the world. Romance! Romance! I walked 15 miles through mud and up and down mountains, and swam three rivers, to get this boat. But if ever you miss me, suddenly, one day, from lecture-room B in King's, or from the Moulin d'Or at lunch, you'll know that I've got sick for the full moon on these little thatched roofs, and the palms against the morning, and the Samoan boys and girls diving thirty feet into a green sea or a deep mountain pool under a waterfall—and that I've gone back."

The next place was Fiji, where he wrote to Edmund Gosse from Suva on November 19th. "I've just got into this place, from Samoa. I said to myself, 'Fiji is obviously the wildest place I can get to round here. The name, and pictures of the inhabitants, prove it.' And lo! a large English town, with two banks, several churches, dental surgeons, a large gaol, auctioneers, book-makers, two newspapers, and all the other appur-tenances of civilisation! But I fancy I'll be able to get some little boat and go off to some smaller wilder islands. . . . . . .

"Perplexing country! At home everything is so simple, and choice is swift, for the sensible man. There is only the choice between writing a good sonnet and making a million pounds. Who could hesitate? But *here* the choice is between writing a sonnet, and climbing a straight hundred-foot cocoanut palm, or diving forty feet from a rock into pellucid blue-green water. Which is the better, there? One's European literary soul begins to be haunted by strange doubts and shaken with fundamental, fantastic misgivings. I think I shall return home. . . . . . .

"Oh, it's horribly true, what you wrote, that one only finds in the South Seas what one brings there. Perhaps I could have found Romance if I'd brought it. Yet I do not think one could help but find *less* trouble than one brings. The idea of the South Seas as a place of passion and a Mohammedan's paradise is but a sailor's yarn. It is nothing near so disturbing. It's rather the opposite of alcohol according to the Porter's definition: for it promotes performance but takes away desire. Yet I can understand Stevenson finding—as you put it—the Shorter Catechism there. One keeps realising, however unwillingly, responsibility. I noticed in myself, and in the other white people in Samoa, a trait that

I have remarked in Schoolmasters. You know
that sort of slightly irritated tolerance, and lack
of *irresponsibility,* that mark the pedagogue?
One feels that one's a White Man (*vide* Kipling
passim)—ludicrously. I kept thinking I was in
the Sixth at Rugby again. These dear good
people, with their laughter and friendliness and
crowns of flowers—one feels that one *must* pro-
tect them. If one was having an evening out
with Falstaff and Bardolph themselves, and a
small delightful child came up with 'Please I'm
lost and I want to get home,' wouldn't one have
to leave good fellowship and spend the evening
in mean streets tracking its abode? That's, I
fancy, how the white man feels in these forgotten
—and dissolving—pieces of heaven. And that
perhaps is what Stevenson felt—I don't know
enough about him. His memory is sweet there,
in Samoa: especially among the natives. The
white men, mostly traders, who remain from his
time, have—for such people—very warm recol-
lections of his personality: but—with a touch
of pathos—avow themselves unable to see any
merit in his work. Such stuff as the *Wrong
Box* they frankly can't understand a grown man
writing . . . I went up the steep hill above
Vailima, where the grave is. It's a high and
lonely spot. I took a Samoan of about 20 to

guide me. He was much impressed by Stevenson's fame. 'That fellow,' he said, 'I think every fellow in world know him.' Then he looked perplexed. 'But my father say,' he went on, 'Stevenson no big man—small man.' That a slight man of medium height should be so famous, puzzled him altogether. If he had been seven feet high, now! Fame is a curious thing. . . . . . . Oh, *do* forgive the envelope. My own, in this awful climate, are all fast stuck, though never filled, like an English churchman's mind. And I'm reduced to these fantastic affairs."

Other letters add touches to his picture. To me he wrote: "Suva is a queer place; much civilised; full of English people who observe the Rules of Etiquette, and call on third Thursdays, and do not speak to the 'natives.' Fiji's not so attractive as Samoa, but more *macabre*. Across the bay are ranges of inky, sinister mountains, over which there are always clouds and darkness. No matter how fine or windy or hot or cheerful it may be in Suva, that trans-sinutic region is nothing but forbidding and terrible. The Greeks would have made it the entrance of the other world—it is just what I've always imagined Avernus to be like. I'm irresistibly attracted by them, and when I come back from my cruise, I intend to walk among them. Shall I return?

If not, spill some blood in a trench—you'll find the recipe in Homer—and my wandering shade will come for an hour or two to lap it. . . . . . . The sunsets here! the colour of the water over the reef! the gloom and terror of those twisted mountains! and the extraordinary contrasts in the streets and the near country—for there are fifty thousand Hindoos, indentured labour, here, emaciated and proud, in Liberty-coloured garments, mournful, standing out among these gay, pathetic, sturdy children the Fijians. The Hindoos, who were civilised when we were Fijians; and the Fijians, who will never be civilised. And amongst them, weedy Australian clerks, uncertain whether they most despise a 'haw-haw Englishman' or a 'dam nigger,' and without the conscience of the one or the charm of the other; secret devil-worshippers, admirers of America, English without tradition and Yankees without go. *Give* me a landed gentry, ten shillings on wheat, and hanging for sheep-stealing; also the Established Church, whence I spring."

To Denis Browne he wrote about the dancing and the music: "I prefer watching a *Siva-Siva* to observing Nijinsky. Oh dear, I so wish you'd been with me for some of these native dances. I've got no ear, and can't get the tunes down. They're very simple—just a few bars with a scale

of about 5 notes, repeated over and over again.
But it's the *Rhythm* that gets you. They get
extraordinarily rhythmic effects, everybody beating their hands, or tapping with a stick; and the
dancers swaying their bodies and tapping with
their feet. None of that damned bounding and
pirouetting. Just *stylisierte* pantomime, sometimes slightly indecent. But *most* exciting.
Next time I get sick of England, I'm going to
bring you along out here, and work the whole
thing out.

"You won't know me when—if ever—I return.
Many things I have lost; my knowledge of art
and literature, my fragmentary manners, my
acquaintance with the English tongue, and any
slight intelligence I ever had; but I have gained
other things; a rich red-brown for my skin, a
knowledge of mixed drinks, an ability to talk or
drink with any kind of man, and a large *réper-
toire* of dirty stories. Am I richer or poorer?
I don't know. I only regret that I shall never
be able to mix in your or any intelligent circles
again. I am indistinguishable (except by my
poverty) from a Hall man."

"Dear Miss Asquith," [1] he wrote in mid-De-
cember from 'somewhere in the mountains of
Fiji.' "Forgive this paper. Its limpness is be-

[1] Miss Violet Asquith, now Lady Bonham-Carter.

cause it has been in terrific thunderstorms, and through most of the rivers in Fiji, in the last few days. Its marks of dirt are because small naked brown babies *will* crawl up and handle it. *And any blood-stains will be mine.* The point is, will they . . .? It's absurd, I know. It's twenty years since they've eaten anybody, and far more since they've done what I particularly and unreasonably detest—fastened the victim down, cut pieces off him one by one, and cooked and eaten them before his eyes. To witness 'one's own transubstantiation into a naked black man, that seems the last indignity. Consideration of the thoughts that pour through the mind of the ever-diminishing remnant of a man, as it sees its late limbs cooking, moves me deeply. I have been meditating a sonnet, as I sit here, surrounded by dusky faces and gleaming eyes:—

Dear, they have poached the eyes you loved so well—

It'd do well for No. 101 and last, in a modern sonnet-sequence, wouldn't it? I don't know how it would go on. The fourth line would have to be

And all my turbulent lips are *maître-d'hôtel*—

I don't know how to scan French. I fancy that limps. But '*all*' is very strong in the modern style.

"The idea comes out in a slighter thing:—

> The limbs that erstwhile charmed your sight
> Are now a savage's delight;
> The ear that heard your whispered vow
> Is one of many *entrées* now;
> Broiled are the arms in which you clung,
> And devilled is the angelic tongue: . . .
> And oh! my anguish as I see
> A Black Man gnaw your favourite knee!
> Of the two eyes that were your ruin,
> One now observes the other stewing.
> My lips (the inconstancy of man!)
> Are yours no more. The legs that ran
> Each dewy morn their love to wake,
> Are now a steak, are now a steak! . . .

Oh, dear! I suppose it ought to end on the Higher Note, the Wider Outlook. Poetry has to, they tell me. You may caress details, all the main parts of the poem, but at last you have to open the window and turn to God, or Earth, or Eternity, or any of the Grand Old Endings. It gives Uplift, as we Americans say. And that's so essential. (Did you ever notice how the Browning family's poems all refer suddenly to God in the last line? It's laughable if you read through them in that way. 'What if that friend happened to be—God?' 'What comes next? Is it—God?' 'And with God be the rest.' 'And if God choose, I shall but love thee better

after death.' . . . etc., etc. I forget them all
now. It shows what the Victorians were.)
  "So must I soar:—

> O love, O loveliest and best,
> · Natives this *body* may digest;
> Whole, and still yours, my *soul* shall dwell,
> Uneaten, safe, incoctible . . .

It's too dull. I shall go out and wander through
the forest paths by the grey moonlight. Fiji in
moonlight is like nothing else in this world or
the next. It's all dim colours and all scents.
And here, where it's high up, the most fantas-
tically-shaped mountains in the world tower up
all around, and little silver clouds and wisps of
mist run bleating up and down the valleys and
hillsides like lambs looking for their mother.
There's only one thing on earth as beautiful; and
that's Samoa by moonlight. That's utterly different, merely Heaven, sheer loveliness. You
lie on a mat in a cool Samoan hut, and look out
on the white sand under the high palms, and a
gentle sea, and the black line of the reef a mile
out, and moonlight over everything, floods and
floods of it, not sticky, like Honolulu moonlight,
not to be eaten with a spoon, but flat and abundant, such that you could slice thin golden-white
shavings off it, as off cheese. And then among

it all are the loveliest people in the world, moving and dancing like gods and goddesses, very quietly and mysteriously, and utterly content. It is sheer beauty, so pure that it's difficult to breathe in it—like living in a Keats world, only it's less syrupy—Endymion without sugar. Completely unconnected with this world.

"There is a poem:

I know an Island
Where the long scented holy nights pass slow,
And there, 'twixt lowland and highland,
The white stream falls into a pool I know,
Deep, hidden with ferns and flowers, soft as dreaming,
Where the brown laughing dancing bathers go . . .

It ends after many pages:

I know an Island
Where the slow fragrant-breathing nights creep past;
And there, 'twixt lowland and highland,
A deep, fern-shrouded, murmurous water glimmers;
There I'll come back at last,
And find my friends, the flower-crowned, laughing swim-
    mers,
And—[1]

I forget. And I've not written the middle part. And it's very bad, like all true poems. I love England; and all the people in it; but oh, how

[1] These lines appear again, considerably altered, in the essay called *Some Niggers*, printed in *Letters from America*.

can one know of heaven on earth and not come back to it? I'm afraid I shall slip away from that slithery, murky place you're (I suppose) in now, and return— Ridiculous.

"I continue in a hot noon, under an orange tree. We rose at dawn and walked many miles and swam seven large rivers and picked and ate many oranges and pineapples and drank cocoa-nuts. Now the two 'boys' who carry my luggage are asleep in the shade. They're Fijians of twenty-three or so who know a few words of English. One of them is the finest-made man I've ever seen; like a Greek statue come to life; strong as ten horses. To see him strip and swim a half-flooded river is an immortal sight.

"Last night we stayed in the house of a moun-tain chief who has spasmodic yearnings after civilisation. When these grow strong, he sends a runner down to the coast to buy any illustrated papers he can find. He knows no English, but he pastes his favourite pictures up round the wall and muses over them. I lectured on them— fragments of the *Sketch* and *Sphere* for several years—to a half-naked reverent audience last night (through my interpreter of course). The Prince of Wales, looking like an Oxford under-graduate, elbows two ladies who display 1911 spring-fashions. A golf champion in a most contorted position occupies a central place. He is regarded, I fancy, as a rather potent and violent deity. To his left is 'Miss Viola Tree, as Eurydice,' to his right Miss Lillah M'Carthy as Jocasta, looking infinitely Mycenaean. I explained about incest, shortly, and Miss M'C. rose tremendously in Fijian estimation. Why do people like their gods to be so eccentric, always? I fancy I left an impression that she was Mr. H. H. Hilton's (is that right? You're a golfer) mother and wife. It is so hard to explain our civilisation to simple people. Anyhow, I disturbed their theology and elevated Lillah to the top place. How Eurydice came in puzzled them and me. I fancy they regard her as a Holy Ghostess, in some sort.

"It's very perplexing. These people—Samoans and Fijians—are so much nicer, and so *much* better-mannered, than oneself. They are stronger, beautifuller, kindlier, more hospitable and courteous, greater lovers of beauty, and even wittier, than average Europeans. And they are—under our influence—a dying race. We gradually fill their lands with plantations and Indian coolies. The Hawaians, up in the Sandwich Islands, have almost altogether gone, and their arts and music with them, and their

islands are a replica of America. A cheerful
thought, that all these places are to become indistinguishable from Denver and Birmingham
and Stuttgart, and the people of dress and be-
haviour precisely like Herr Schmidt, and Mr.
Robinson, and Hiram O. Guggenheim. And
now they're so . . . it's impossible to describe
how far nearer the Kingdom of Heaven—or the
Garden of Eden—these good, naked, laughing
people are than oneself or one's friends. . . .
But I forget. You are an anti-socialist, and I
mustn't say a word against our modern indus-
trial system. I beg your pardon.

"I go down to the coast to catch a boat to New
Zealand, where I shall post this. Thence to
Tahiti, to hunt for lost Gauguins. Then back
to barbarism in America. God knows when I
shall get home. In the spring, I hope. Is England still there? Forgive this endless scrawl.

"I suppose you're rushing from lunch-party
to lunch-party, and dance to dance, and opera
to political platform. Won't you come and
learn how to make a hibiscus-wreath for your
hair, and sail a canoe, and swim two minutes
under water catching turtles, and dive forty feet
into a waterfall, and climb a cocoanut-palm?
It's more worth while."

Sometimes the desire for England and his friends came uppermost. "I'd once thought it necessary to marry," he wrote to Jacques Raverat from Fiji. "I *approve* of marriage for the world. I think you're all quite right, so don't be alarmed. But not for me. I'm too old. The Point of Marriage is Peace—to work in. But can't one get it otherwise? Why, certainly when one's old. And so I will. I know what things are good: friendship and work and conversation. These I shall have. How one can fill life, if one's energetic and knows how to dig! I have thought of a thousand things to do, in books and poems and plays and theatres and societies and housebuilding and dinner-parties, when I get Home. We shall have fun. Now we have so painfully achieved middle-age, shall we not reap the fruits of that achievement, my dyspeptic friend? By God, yes! Will you come and walk with me in Spain next summer? And will you join me on the Poet's Round?—a walk I've planned. One starts from Charing Cross, in a south-easterly direction, and calls on de la Mare at Anerley, and finds Davies at Sevenoaks—a day's march to Belloc at King's Head, then up to Wibson [1] on the borders of Gloucestershire, back by Stratford, Rugby, and

[1] Wilfrid Gibson.

the Chilterns, where Masefield and Chesterton dwell. Wouldn't it give one a queer idea of England?

"Three months a year I am going to live with you and Gwen, three with Dudley and Anne, three with the Ranee,[1] and three alone. A perfect life. I almost catch the next boat to 'Frisco at the thought of it." (At this point in the letter there is a constellation of blots, explained as 'Tears of Memory.')

"There is nothing in the world like friendship. And there is no man who has had such friends as I, so many, so fine, so various, so multiform, so prone to laughter, so strong in affection, and so permanent, so trustworthy, so courteous, so stern with vices and so blind to faults or folly, of such swiftness of mind and strength of body, so apt both to make jokes and to understand them. Also their faces are beautiful, and I love them. I repeat a long list of their names every night before I sleep. Friendship is always exciting, and yet always safe. There is no lust in it, and therefore no poison. It is cleaner than love, and older; for children and very old people have friends, but they do not love. It gives more and takes less, it is fine in the enjoying, and without pain when absent, and it leaves only good memo-

---

[1] His name for his mother.

ries. In love all laughter ends with an ache, but laughter is the very garland on the head of friendship. I will not love, and I will not be loved. But I will have friends round me continually, all the days of my life, and in whatever lands I may be. So we shall laugh and eat and sing, and go great journeys in boats and on foot, and write plays and perform them, and pass innumerable laws taking their money from the rich. . . . I err. I praise too extravagantly, conveying an impression that friendship always gives peace. And even at the moment I feel a hunger, too rending for complete peace, to see all your faces again and to eat food with you."

Home thoughts from abroad of a different order were sent to Miss Nesbitt:—"I see I'm going to have the hell of an uncomfortable life," he wrote. "I want too many different things. I keep now pining after London. I want to talk, talk, talk. Is there anything better in the world than sitting at a table and eating good food and drinking great drink, and discussing everything under the sun with wise and brilliant people? . . . . . .

"Oh but I'm going to have such a time when I get back. I'm going to have the loveliest rooms in King's, and I'm going to spend 5 days a week there, and 3 in London (that's 8, stoopid), and in King's I'm going to entertain all the mad and lovely people in the world, and I'm never going to sit down to dinner without a philosopher, a poet, a musician, an actress, a dancer, and a bishop at table with me. I'm going to get up such performances as will turn Cambridge upside down. I'm going to have Yeats and Cannan and Craig and Barker to give a lecture each on modern drama. I'm going to have my great play in the Grantchester garden. I'm going— oh, hell, I don't know what I'm going to do— but every morning I shall drift up and down the backs in a punt, discussing anything in the world with anybody who desires."

He left Fiji in December. "Life's been getting madder and madder," he wrote from Auckland on December 17th. "I tumbled into Fiji without a friend or an introduction, and left it a month later amidst the loud grief of the united population, white and black. The two 'boys' (aged 23 or 24) I took with me when I went walking through the centre of the island, to carry my bags, are my sworn and eternal friends. One of them ('Ambele,' under which I, but not you, can recognise 'Abel') was six foot high, very broad, and more perfectly made than any man or statue I have ever seen. His grin stretched from ear to ear. And he could carry me across rivers (when I was tired of swimming them, for we crossed vast rivers every mile or two) for a hundred yards or so, as. I should carry a box of matches. I think of bringing him back with me as a servant or bodyguard to England. He loved me because, though I was far weaker than he, I was far braver. The Fijians are rather cowards. And on precipices I am peculiarly reckless. The boys saved me from rolling off to perdition about thirty times, and respected me for it, though thinking me insane. What would you say if I turned up with two vast cannibal servants, black-skinned and perpetually laughing—all of us attired only in loin-cloths, and red flowers in our hair? I think I should be irresistible.

"Why, precisely, I'm here, I don't know. I seem to have missed a boat somewhere, and I can't get on to Tahiti till the beginning of January. Damn. And I hear that a man got to Tahiti two months ahead of me, and found—and carried off—some Gauguin paintings on glass. DAMN!

"New Zealand turns out to be in the midst of summer, and almost exactly like England. I eat strawberries, large garden strawberries, every day; and it's the middle of December! It feels curiously unnatural, perverse, like some frightful vice out of Havelock Ellis. I blush and eat secretively. I'll describe New Zealand another day. It's a sort of Fabian England, very upper-middle-class and gentle and happy (after Canada), no poor, and the Government owning hotels and running char-à-bancs. All the women smoke, and dress very badly, and nobody drinks. Everybody seems rather ugly— but perhaps that's compared with the South Seas."

The Englishness of New Zealand made home affairs vivid to him again, and he wrote vehemently to his mother about the Dublin Strike. "I feel wild about Dublin. I always feel in strikes that 'the men are always right,' as a man says in *Clayhanger*. Of course the poor are always right against the rich, though often enough the men are in the wrong over some point of the moment (it's not to be wondered at). But Dublin seems to be one of the clearest cases on record. . . . . . . When the *Times* begins saying that the employers are in the wrong, they must be very unpardonably and rottenly so indeed. I do hope people are contributing for the wives and children in Dublin. Could you send two guineas in my name? I'll settle when I get back. But I'd like it done immediately. I expect you will have sent some yourself. . . . . . .

"The queer thing [about New Zealand]," he goes on, "is that they've got all the things in the Liberal or mild Fabian programme:—eight hour day (and less), bigger old age pensions, access to the land, minimum wage, insurance, etc., etc., and yet it's not Paradise. The same troubles exist in much the same form (except that there's not much bad poverty). Cost of living is rising quicker than wages. There are the same troubles between unions and employers, and between rich and poor. I suppose there'll be no peace anywhere till the rich are curbed altogether."

On the voyage from New Zealand to Tahiti he made great friends with a Lancashire business man, Mr. Harold Ashworth, who wrote after his death to Mrs. Brooke. The letters show the kind of impression that he made on those who met him at this time. "I am happy to believe," says Mr. Ashworth, "that he and I became real friends, and many a time I would invoke his aid when my rather aggressive Radicalism brought the 'Smoke-room' men at me *en masse*. I never met so entirely likeable a chap, and when I could 'get him going' about his wanderings, or provoke him into discussions about Literature, I was one walking ear! . . . . . . I almost wept to know I could never again see that golden head and kindly smile—'Young Apollo,' I used to dub him in my mind, whilst the fresh wind tossed his hair, and his boyish eyes lit up with pleasure at some of my anecdotes of strange people and places. . . . . . . Your son was not merely a genius; what is perhaps more important, he had a charm that was literally like Sunshine. To say his manner was *perfect* is putting it quite inadequately. . . . . . . His·memory is blessed by hundreds of men like me who were so fortunate as to meet him and were the better for that happy adventure."

Another friend made on his travels was Reginald Berkeley, who was his chief companion on his excursions in Fiji. Rupert sent him from the s.s. *Niagara* a long letter about the tec..nique of writing. "One can only advise people two or three years younger," he says. "Beyond that, one has forgotten." The end of it shows him insisting on the importance for artists of the attitude which he had recommended for everyone in his letter to Ben Keeling of three years before. "Finally," he says, "I charge you, be kind to life; and do not bruise her with the bludgeon of the *a priori*. Poor dirty woman, she responds to sympathy. Sympathetic imagination with everybody and everything is the artist's one duty. He should be one with every little clergyman, and the stockbroker's most secret hope should be his hope. In the end, the words of Strindberg's heroine are the only motto, 'The race of man is greatly to be pitied.' Isn't that true? Hatred should be given out sparingly. It's too valuable to use carelessly. And, misused, it prevents understanding. And it is our duty to understand; for if we don't, no one else will."

His next stay was about three months in Tahiti. "I've decided to stay here another month," he wrote to Miss Nesbitt in February, "for two very good reasons: (1) that I haven't enough money to get out, (2) that I've found the most ideal place in the world to live and work in.[1] A wide verandah over a blue lagoon, a wooden pier with deep clear water for diving, and coloured fish that swim between your toes. There also swim between your toes, more or less, scores of laughing brown babies from two years to fourteen. Canoes and boats, rivers, fishing with spear net and line, the most wonderful food in the world—strange fishes and vegetables perfectly cooked. Europe slides from me terrifyingly. . . . . Will it come to your having to

[1] This was at Mataiea, about 30 miles from the chief town, Papeete.

fetch me? The boat's ready to start; the brown lovely people in their bright clothes are gathered on the old wharf to wave her away. Everyone has a white flower behind their ear. Mamua has given me one. Do you know the significance of a white flower worn over the ear? A white flower over the right ear means 'I am looking for a sweetheart.' And a white flower over the left ear means 'I have found a sweetheart.' And a white flower over each ear means 'I have one sweetheart, and am looking for another.' A white flower over each ear, my dear, is dreadfully the most fashionable way of adorning yourself in Tahiti.

"*Bon voyage* to the travellers. Good luck to everybody else. Love to the whole world. Tonight we will put scarlet flowers in our hair, and sing strange slumbrous South Sea songs to the concertina, and drink red French wine, and dance, and bathe in a soft lagoon by moonlight, and eat great squelchy tropical fruits, custard-apples, papaia, pomegranate, mango, guava and the rest. *Urana.* I have a million lovely and exciting things to tell you—but not now."

How thoroughly he became imbued with the life, the feeling, and the philosophy of the islands, appears from a sociological epistle which he wrote to Jacques Raverat after his return to England. "As for Land, my Frog, we must have a great deal held in common. It is good for men to work *of* themselves, but not too much *for* themselves. In my part of the world, if we want to build a canoe, we all put wreaths in our hair, and take the town hatchet, and Bill's axe, and each his own hunting-knife, and have a bit of pig each for luck, and a drink, and go out. And as we go we sing. And when we have got to a large tree we sit round it. And the two biggest men take the axes and hit the tree in turn. And the rest of us beat our hands rhythmically and sing a song saying 'That is a tree—cut down the tree—we will make a boat,' and so on. And when those two are tired, they drink and sit, and other two take their places . . . and later the hollowing of the canoe, and the fashioning of an out-rigger, and the making of benches and the shaping of paddles. And when all's done, we go home and sing all night, and dance a great deal. For we have another canoe.

"And when you have got a lot of other Goddites together and started to build a Cathedral, why, you'll see what fun it is working together, instead of in a dirty little corner alone, suspicious, greedy, competitive, hating all the world, like a modern artist or a French peasant or a money-lender or a golfer."

He had begun writing verse again, and in the 'wide verandah' he wrote or finished *Tiare Tahiti,*[1] *Retrospect,* and the *Great Lover,*[2] which he sent me (he had appointed me his 'literary agent or grass-executor' during his travels)[3] for *New Numbers.* This publication had been planned in July by correspondence with Lascelles Abercrombie, John Drinkwater and Wilfrid Gibson. They meant at first to call it *The Gallows Garland,* after The Gallows, Abercrombie's cottage in Gloucestershire, from which it was to be published; and Rupert thought the change very stupid. He had sketched the contents of the first number. Abercrombie was to contribute a short epic on *Asshurbanipal and Nebuchadnezzar,* Drinkwater an ode called *The Sonority of God,* and Gibson two narrative

---

[1] A postscript to a letter to his mother elucidates a line in this poem. "They call me *Pupure* here—it means 'fair' in Tahitian—because I have fair hair!"

[2] Speculation has been aroused by the line in this poem praising 'the comfortable smell of friendly fingers.' When asked *whose* fingers, he said his nurse's; and admitted that it might have been the soap.

[3] He took large views of my duties. "Damn it," he had written from Vancouver, "what's the good of a friend if he can't sit down and write off a few poems for one at a pinch? That's what I count on your doing, if the editors press."

I hope this note will not start a vain hunt for *spuria* among the published poems.

poems, *Poor Bloody Bill* and *The Brave Poor Thing*, *from a series named Gas-Stoves.* Rupert himself did not expect to manage more than one sonnet, to be entitled *Oh dear! Oh dear!* The first number came out in February 1914; and after three more issues it was discontinued because of the war, before his death had broken the fair companionship.

To illustrate his method of work at this time, it may be of interest to print the first draft of the *Psychical Research* sonnet, with his corrections:

> *, when we're beyond the sun,*
> Not with vain tears we'll beat, when all is done,
> *We'll beat*
> Unheard on the substantial doors, nor tread
> *aimless*
> Those dusty high-roads of the wandering Dead
> *Plaintive for Earth; but rather turn and run*
> Remembering Earth. We'll turn, I think, and run
> Down some close-covered by-way of the air,
> *Some*
> Or low sweet alley between wind and wind,
> *Stoop under faint gleams, thread the shadows, find*
> Pull down the shadows over us, and find
> *Some*
> A whispering ghost-forgotten nook, and there
> Spend in pure converse our eternal day;
> Think each in each, immediately wise;

Learn all we lacked before, hear, know, and say
What this tumultuous body now denies;
And feel, who have laid our groping hands away;
And see, no longer blinded by our eyes.[1]

But to return to Tahiti. "I've been ill," he wrote to me on March 7th. "I got some beastly coral-poisoning into my legs, and a local microbe on the top of that, and made the places worse by neglecting them, and sea-bathing all day (which turns out to be the worst possible thing). I was in the country when it came on bad, and tried native remedies, which took all the skin off, and produced such a ghastly appearance that I hurried into town. . . . . . . I've got over it now, and feel very spry. I'm in a hovel at the back of the hotel, and contemplate the yard. The extraordinary life of the place flows round and through my room—for here no one, man or woman, scruples to come through one's room at any moment, if it happens to be a short cut. By day nothing much happens in the yard—except

[1] Though there are no changes in the concluding lines, I print them for the sake of a parallel, shown me by John Drinkwater, in Andrew Marvell's *Dialogue between Soul and Body*, where Soul says:

O, who shall from this dungeon raise
A soul enslaved so many ways,
With bolts of bones, that fettered stands
In feet, and manacled in hands;
Here blinded with an eye, and there
Deaf with the drumming of an ear?

when a horse tried to eat a hen the other afternoon. But by night, after ten, it's filled with flit-
ting figures of girls, with wreaths of white flowers, keeping assignations. Occasionally two
rivals meet, and fill the darker corners with cur-
sings and scratchings. Or occasionally a youth
intercepts a faithless lady, and has a pretty oper-
atic scene under my window. It is all—all Papeete—like a Renaissance Italy, with the venom
taken out. No, simpler, light-come and light-go,
passionate and forgetful, like children, and all
the time South Pacific, that is to say unmalicious
and good-tempered. . . . . . .

"I really do feel a little anchorless. I shall
be glad to be back among you all, and tied to
somewhere in England. I'll never, never, never
go to sea again. All I want in life is a cottage,
and leisure to write supreme poems and plays.
I can't do it in this vagabondage."

I don't know what happened between this letter and the next to produce the gloom it shows
about his work. He had always, at school and
onwards, been apt to have fits of thinking that
he would never write again, but this time the
foreboding seems more serious than usual. He
begins cheerfully 'some time in March': "It's *so*
funny; getting a letter of January 25, and not
having heard anything from anybody since Octo-

ber. Your letter of November, announcing
your marriage with [someone very improbable];
your kindly Christmas information about the
disastrous fire in Bilton Road and the disposal
of the Ranee's and Alfred's cinders; your New
Year's epistle announcing your, Wilfrid's and
Albert's Knighthoods; the later letter that re-
counted your conversations with Shaw, the
Earthquake, the War with Germany, the Chinese
Ballet, Stravinsky's comic opera, the new El
Greco, Gilbert [Cannan]'s trial, Masefield's
latest knock-about farce, Arthur Benson's duel
. . . all these I have not yet had.   They await
me in 'Frisco.   So I take up the threads at the
25th of January—now itself some way down in
the heap of yesterday's seven thousand years—
and study them rather confusedly.   Flecker—
Wilfrid—poetry—plays—Moulin d'Or—*Hullo
Tango!* they all stir, these names, some dusty
memories away in the back of my subconsciousness.   Somewhere they must have meant something to me, in another life.   A vision of taxis
slides across the orange and green of the sunset.
For a moment the palms dwindle to lamp-posts.

> So a poor ghost beside his misty streams
> Is haunted by strange doubts and fugitive dreams,
> Hints of a pre-Lethean life, of men,
> Rocks, stars, and skin, things unintelligible,

> And the sun on waving grass—he knows not when,
> And feet that ran, but where, he cannot tell.[1]

(You recognise the master-hand?)

"I must come back and see if I can take to it again. Plan out a life for me for next year, Eddie. (Here follows another sketch for living at Cambridge, much the same as the one already given.) The other half of the week I shall reside with you—I warn you.

"But, my dear, I doubt if you'll have me. The Game is Up, Eddie. If I've gained facts through knocking about with Conrad characters in a Gauguin *entourage,*—I've lost a dream or two. I tried to be a poet. And because I'm a clever writer, and because I was forty times as sensitive as anybody else, I succeeded a little. *Es ist vorüber; es ist unwiederruflich zu Ende.* I am what I came out here to be. Hard, quite, quite hard. I have become merely a minor character in a Kipling story.

"I'll never be able to write anything more, I think; or perhaps I can do plays of a sort. . . . I think I'll have to manage a theatre. I feel very energetic; and very capable. Is that a great come-down? I think that what I really feel like is living. I want to talk and talk and

---

[1] An unrevised form of part of the sonnet *Hauntings.*

talk . . . and in the intervals have extraordinary adventures. Perhaps this, too, is a come-down. But haven't I, at 26, reached the age when one should begin to learn? An energy that had rushed on me with the cessation of my leprous skin-disease, and the approaching end of six months' peace of soul, is driving me furiously on. This afternoon I go fishing in a canoe with a native girl on a green and purple reef. Tonight from ten to two, spearing fish in the same lagoon by torchlight. Tomorrow at dawn, up into the mountains on foot with a mad Englishman, four natives, and a half-caste, to a volcanic lake in the interior. There we build a house and stay for two days. The natives return, and the M.E. and myself push on for and pass down to the other coast. Perhaps we get it. Perhaps not.

"In any case we hope to see some ghosts— they abound in the interior. They come to you by night, and as you watch them their bellies burst, and their entrails fall to the ground, and their eyes—unpupilled balls of white—fall out too, and they stink and shine. This morning I've been reading *The Triumph of Time,* and *Bartholomew Fair.* . . . . . .

"Learning, learning, learning. . . . Is there anything else to do except *taste?* Will you come with me to Morocco, Persia, Russia, Egypt,

Abyssinia, and the Aran Islands? I'm afraid I shan't be able to settle down at home. It'll be an advantage that I can come to England through America. For then, I'll find it so lovely that I won't be hankering after sunlight and brown people and rainbow-coloured fish. At least, I won't for some months, or a year.

"I'll learn at home, a bit. There's so much to learn there—if only one's sensible enough to know it. And I feel hard enough to make the attempt. I want to love my friends and hate my enemies, again. Both greatly—but not *too* much. Which brings me round to [an enemy] and Clubs. . . . . . . I want a club to take an occasional stranger into, for a drink, and to read the papers in, and sometimes to have a quiet meal in. Where do you think I should go? I want somewhere I needn't always be spick and span in, and somewhere I don't have to pay a vast sum. Alas, why are there no decent clubs? What do the jolly people all do? I want to belong to the same club as de la Mare. Where does de la Mare go? To Anerley, S.E., I suppose.

> There was once a-metrist of Anerley,
> Whose neighbours were mundane but mannerly.
> > They don't cavil the least
> > At a stray anapæst,
> But they *do* bar his spondees in Anerley.

I'll post this and send off my bundle of MSS. from 'Frisco.''

He left Tahiti in April. "Last night," he wrote on the steamer, "I looked for the Southern Cross as usual, and looked for it in vain—like the moon for Omar Khayyam—it had gone down below the horizon. It is still shining and wheeling for those good brown people in the islands— and they're laughing and kissing and swimming and dancing beneath it—but for me it is set; and I don't know that I shall ever see it again. It's queer. I was sad at heart to leave Tahiti. But I resigned myself to the vessel, and watched the green shores and rocky peaks fade with hardly a pang. I had told so many of those that loved me, so often, 'oh yes, I'll come back—next year perhaps, or the year after'—that I suppose I'd begun to believe it myself. It was only yesterday, when I knew that the Southern Cross had left me, that I suddenly realised I had left behind those lovely places and lovely people, perhaps for ever. I reflected that there was surely nothing else like them in this world, and very probably nothing in the next, and that I was going far away from gentleness and beauty and kindliness, and the smell of the lagoons, and the thrill of that dancing, and the scarlet of the flamboyants, and the white and gold of other flowers; and that I was going to America, which is full of harshness and hideous sights, and ugly people, and civilisation, and corruption, and bloodiness, and all evil. So I wept a little, and very sensibly went to bed. . . . . . .

"Certain reprehensible corners of my heart whisper to me, 'There's a village in Samoa, with the moonlight on the beach'—or 'I've heard of a hill in Japan'—or 'one said there's an inn in Thibet over a sheer precipice'—or 'the Victoria Nyanza is an attractive lake'—or 'that trail in the North-West up the Mackenzie—Morris said he'd go whenever I wanted'—or 'I wonder if it's true about that flower in the Andes that smells like no other flower upon earth, and when once a man has smelt it he can't but return there to live in those hills in the end, though he come back from the ends of the earth.' . . . . . .

"I'll be Wordsworth's lark, that soars but doesn't roam, true to the kindred points of heaven and home. These scraps of English poetry start whispering within me—that means I'm North of the Equator, doesn't it? It's a good sign, perhaps. English thoughts are waking in me. They'll fetch me back. Call me home, I pray you. I've been away long enough. I'm older than I was. I've left bits of me about —some of my hair in Canada, and one skin in

Honolulu, and another in Fiji, and a bit of a third in Tahiti, and half a tooth in Samoa, and bits of my heart all over the place. I'm deader than I was. *Partir, c'est toujours mourir un peu* —you know that admirable and true proverb, don't you? A little old Frenchman, a friend of mine, told it me as we leaned over the rail and watched the waving crowds and the red roofs and the hills and the clouds dwindle and vanish. He was going home to France for a year for his health. 'Home,' he'd be angry at that. *'Mon home c'est ici,'* he told me repeatedly. He is married to a native woman these fifteen years—no children of his own, but plenty adopted. She was so much finer than a white woman, he sighed—so lovely, so faithful, so competent, so charming and happy, and so extraordinarily intelligent. I told him what Tagore told me about white women compared with Indian, and he gave me his observations, and we entirely agreed, and forgot our sorrows in inventing bilingual insults to the swarms of ugly American and Colonial girls on board."

"Oh, God! Oh, God!" his next letter to me began, from San Francisco in April. "How I hate civilisation and houses and trams and collars." But the shock was tempered to him. "I've found good friends in the quieter parts of this region, who live in a garden filled with roses and hyacinths and morning-glory. So I'll rest a day or two and try to get over the effects of my first re-entry into civilisation. And then I'll sneak away East and come home. I want to live in a hut by a river and pretend I'm Polynesian. Will you come and see me o' week's ends? . . . . . . Oh! Oh! I am old as death. *Urania!*" And from the train: "I read books on *Indirect Primaries*,[1] just to get the South Seas out of my blood. One must remember one has trousers on again. I had a faint thought of going to Mexico. But I guess it won't be much of a war. You'll be vanishing for Whitsuntide soon. A yachting trip to Ulster? I do hope you're going to let the Orangemen slit all the priests' throats first; and then shoot *them*. I'll enlist on either side, any day. Your gnostic.   RUPERT."

"It's eleven months," he wrote to Miss Nesbitt from Arizona, "that I've not been looked after, and my clothes are in an awful state, and my hair not cut, and I rarely shave. I'm so tired of it. Comprenny? Do you get me? I shall—(prepare your ears and hold tight)—shall sail from New York on June 6th, and by June 15th I shall

[1] He was also reading Boswell. "I've discovered," he wrote, "that Dr. Johnson is the only man I love. An Englishman, by God!"

be in London. My dear, one thing I would implore you. It's very silly. But don't tell anybody the exact day I'm coming back. It's my fancy to blow in on them unexpected—just to wander into Raymond Buildings and hear Eddie squeak 'Oh, *my dear,* I thought you were in Tahiti!' It's *awfly* silly and romantic, but the thought does give me the keenest and most exquisite pleasure. Don't give away one of the first poets in England—but there is in him still a very very small portion that's just a little childish."

"I have such news," he wrote in his next letter. "It begins with Maurice Browne[1] and his wife going to Europe a week sooner than I had planned to. We squabbled, I saying they should defer their departure a week for the pleasure of going with me; they, ridiculously, that I should hasten my leaving this land some seven days for the honour of their companionship. Neither side would yield; so we parted in wrath. They pettily, I with some dignity. Coming here, I found two engagements fallen through; and last night I dreamed very vividly that I arrived in England, and telephoned to everybody I knew, and they were *awfully* nice, and then went round and saw them, and they were *lovely.* Friends I

[1] Director of the Little Theatre at Chicago.

had known long ago, between whom and myself
evil and pain has come, greeted me in the old
first way; and other friends who have stayed
friends were wonderfully the same; and there
were new friends. . . . . . . I woke laughing and
crying. I felt I *must* get back. I telephoned to
Browne, flew to some agents, and in consequence
I sail from New York on May 29th, and reach
Plymouth—oh blessed name, oh loveliness! Plymouth—was there ever so sweet and droll a
sound? Drake's Plymouth, English Western
Plymouth, city where men speak softly, and
things are sold for shillings, not for dollars; and
there is love, and beauty, and old houses; and beyond which there are little fields, very green,
bounded by small piled walls of stone; and behind them—I know ft—the brown and black,
splintered, haunted moor. By that the train
shall go up; by Dartmouth, where my brother
was—I will make a litany; by Torquay, where
Verrall stayed; and by Paignton, where I have
walked in the rain; past Ilsington, where John
Ford was born, and Appledore, in the inn of
which I wrote a poem against a commercial trav-
eller; by Dawlish, of which John Keats sang;
within sight of Widdicombe, where old Uncle
Tom Cobley rode a mare; not a dozen miles from
John Galsworthy at Manaton; within sight al-

most of that hill at Drewsteignton on which I lay out all one September night, crying—and to Exeter, and to Ottery St. Mary where Coleridge sojourned; and across Wiltshire, where men built and sang many centuries before the Aquila. Oh noble train, oh glorious and forthright and English train! I will look round me at the English faces, and out at the English fields, and I will pray——reach Plymouth, as I was saying when I was interrupted, on Friday, June 5th."

I got wind of his design to arrive like a bolt from the blue, and represented the disaster it would be if he came and found the door closed against him. He yielded, and at 2.45 a.m. on June 6th (for the forthright English train was very late) Denis Browne and I met him at Paddington.

VI

All the old threads were picked up at once. "To the poor stay-at-home," writes Walter de la Mare, "the friend who placidly reappeared from the ends of the earth seemed as little changed as one who gaily and laughingly goes to bed and gaily and laughingly comes down next morning after a perfectly refreshing sleep." He was still exactly the 'Young Apollo' of Mrs. Cornford's

Cambridge epigram; though the glint of quite
peculiarly real shining gold that had always been
in his hair had been tanned out of it by the Southern sun; and though one felt, in a hundred inde-
finable ways, that he was now more than ever
'prepared'; not, as it turned out, for the 'long lit-
tleness of life,' but rather for its brief greatness.

The morning after his return he hurried off to
Rugby for a few days with his mother. Then he
had six crowded, happy weeks, mostly in London, seeing old friends and making new ones—
including Lascelles Abercrombie, whom he met
for the first time, though they had long been
friends by proxy and by correspondence. His
shyness, which had always been a part of his
rather curious modesty and 'unspoiltness,' was
wearing off; and I am told he confessed, on being
asked, that it had now dawned upon him for the
first time that when he came into a room where
there were new people the chances were that they
would like him, rather than not.

At the end of July came the war-cloud—and
then the war. He has described his feelings when
he heard the news in the essay *An Unusual
Young Man* (the setting is imaginary—he was
not returning from a cruise, but staying with the
Cornfords in Norfolk). At first he was just un-

happy and bewildered. "I'm so uneasy—subconsciously," he wrote. "All the vague perils of the time—the world seems so dark—and I'm vaguely frightened. I feel hurt to think that France may suffer. And it hurts, too, to think that Germany may be harmed by Russia. And I'm anxious that England may act rightly. I can't *bear* it if she does wrong."

"I've just been to a music-hall," he wrote early in August. "It was pretty full. Miss C. Loftus was imitating somebody I saw infinite years ago—Elsie Janis—in her imitation of a prehistoric figure called Frank Tinney. God! how far away it all seemed. Then a dreadful cinematographic reproduction of a hand drawing patriotic things—Harry Furniss it was, funny pictures of a soldier and a sailor (at the time I suppose dying in Belgium), a caricature of the Kaiser, greeted with a perfunctory hiss—nearly everyone sat silent. Then a scribbled message was shown: 'War declared with Austria 11,9.' There was a volley of quick, low hand-clapping—more a signal of recognition than anything else. Then we dispersed into Trafalgar Square and bought midnight War editions. . . . In all these days I haven't been so near tears; there was such tragedy and dignity in the people. . . . . . .

"If there's any good in anything I've done, it's made by the beauty and goodness of . . . a few I've known. All these people at the front who are fighting muddledly enough for some idea called England—it's some faint shadowing of goodness and loveliness they have in their hearts to die for."

For the first day or two he did not realise that he must fight—one of his ideas was to go to France and help get in the crops. But before we had been at war a week he was back in London, seeking out the best way to serve as a soldier. "I've spent a fortnight," he wrote on August 24th, "in chasing elusive employment about. For a time I got drilled on the chance of getting into a London corps as a private, but now I really think I shall get a commission. Territorial probably, through Cambridge. The whole thing, and the insupportable stress of this time, tired me to a useless rag."

Early in September Winston Churchill offered him a commission in the Royal Naval Division, then forming; and he and Denis Browne [1] joined

---

[1] I may here briefly commemorate William Denis Browne, whose death at 26 left no monument of his powers, except a few songs of great beauty. He was a musician of rare promise and complete equipment; and I have high authority for saying that his grasp of the foundations and tendencies of modern music was unique. I cannot here describe the singular charm of his character and personality. Enough that he never failed in honour, or in kindness,

the Anson Battalion on September 27th. I saw them off to Betteshanger Camp from Charing Cross—excited and a little shy, like two new boys going to school—happy and handsome in their new uniforms, and specially proud of their caps, which had very superior badges.

The Anson soon went to Chatham for musketry, and there he wrote: "Often enough I feel a passing despair. I mean what you meant—the gulf between non-combatants and combatants. Yet it's not that—it's the withdrawal of combatants into a special seclusion and reserve. We're under a curse—or a blessing, or a vow to be different. The currents of our lives are interrupted. What is it . . . I know—yes. The central purpose of my life, the aim and end of it now, the thing God wants of me, is to get good at beating Germans. That's sure. But that isn't what it *was*. What it was, I never knew; and God knows I never found it. But it reached out deeply for other things than my present need. . . . There *is* the absence. Priests and criminals—we're both—are celibates . . . and so I

or in good sense, or in humour; and there were many who loved him.

He was a friend of Rupert's at Rugby, at Cambridge, and in London; last, his brother-in-arms; and he cared for him, as will be told, in his mortal illness. Six weeks afterwards, on the 4th of June, he followed him, fighting with high gallantry in the attack on the Turkish trenches before Krithia.

feel from my end sometimes that it *is* a long, long way to Tipperary. And yet, all's well. I'm the happiest person in the world."

There were humours in the life; for instance, a false alarm of invasion at Chatham, when "elderly men rushed about pulling down swords from the messroom walls, and fastened them on with safety-pins"; or this incident in the day's routine: "I had to make an inventory the other day of all their kit, to compare with what they *should* have. I soon found that questions about some of the articles on the lists were purely academic. 'How many handkerchiefs have you?' The first two men were prompted to say 'none.' The third was called Cassidy. 'How many phwat, sorr?' 'Handkerchiefs.'—'?'—'Handkerchiefs, man, handkerchiefs.' (*In a hoarse whisper to the Petty Officer*) 'Phwat does he mane?' P.O. (*in a stage whisper*), 'Ter blow yer nose with, yer bloody fool.' Cassidy (*rather indignant*), 'None, sorr!' They were dears, and very strong, some of them."

On the 4th of October they sailed for Antwerp. When it was all over, and he was having a little leave in London, he wrote to a friend: "I've been extremely slack and sleepy these last few days. I think it was the reaction after the excitement. Also I caught *conjunctivitis*, alias pink-eye, in some of the foul places we slept in; and my eyes have been swollen, red, unlovely, exuding a thick plum-tree gum, and very painful. I *hope* they're getting better. . . . . . . It's only a fortnight ago! We were pulled out of bed at 5 a.m. on the Sunday, and told that we started at 9. We marched to Dover, highly excited, only knowing that we were bound for Dunkirk, and supposing that we'd stay there quietly, training, for a month. Old ladies waved handkerchiefs, young ladies gave us apples, and old men and children cheered, and we cheered back, and I felt very elderly and sombre, and full of thought of how human life was a flash between darknesses, and that x per cent of those who cheered would be blown into another world within a few months; and they all seemed to me so innocent and pathetic and noble, and my eyes grew round and tear-stained. . . . . . . [Arrived at Dunkirk] we sat in a great empty shed a quarter of a mile long, waiting for orders. After dark the senior officers rushed round and informed us that we were going to Antwerp, that our train was sure to be attacked, and that if we got through we'd have to sit in trenches till we were wiped out. So we all sat under lights writing last letters, a very tragic and amusing affair. It *did* bring home to me how very futile and unfinished my life was. I felt so angry. I had to imagine, supposing I *was* killed. There was nothing except a vague gesture of good-bye to you and my mother and a friend or two. I seemed so remote and barren and stupid. I seemed to have missed everything.

"We *weren't* attacked that night in the train. So we got out at Antwerp and marched through the streets, and everyone cheered and flung themselves on us, and gave us apples and chocolate and flags and kisses, and cried *Vivent les Anglais* and 'Heep! Heep! Heep!'

"We got out to a place called Vieux Dieux (or something like it) passing refugees and Belgian soldiers by millions. Every mile the noises got louder, immense explosions and detonations. We stopped in the town square at Vieux Dieux; five or six thousand British troops, a lot of Belgians, guns going through, transport-waggons, motorcyclists, orderlies on horses, staff officers, and the rest. An extraordinary and thrilling confusion. As it grew dark the thunders increased, and the sky was lit by extraordinary glares. We were all given entrenching tools. Everybody looked worried. Suddenly our battalion was marched round the corner out of the din, through an old gate in the immense wild garden of a recently-deserted villa-château. There we had to sleep. On the rather dirty and wild-looking sailors trudged, over lawns, through orchards, and across pleasaunces. Little pools glimmered through the trees, and deserted fountains; and round corners one saw, faintly, occasional Cupids and Venuses—a scattered company of rather bad statues—gleaming quietly. The sailors dug their latrines in the various rose-gardens, and lay down to sleep—but it was bitter cold—under the shrubs. By two the shells had got unpleasantly near, and some message came. So up we got—frozen and sleepy—and toiled off through the night. By dawn we got into trenches—very good ones—and relieved Belgians.

"This is *very* dull. And it doesn't really reflect my state of mind. For when I think back on it, my mind is filled with various disconnected images and feelings. And if I could tell you these fully, you *might* find it wonderful, or at least queer. There's the excitement in the trenches (we weren't attacked seriously in our part) with people losing their heads and fussing and snapping. It's queer to see the people who *do* break under the strain of danger and responsibility. It's always the rotten ones. Highly sensitive people don't, queerly enough. I was relieved to find I was incredibly brave! I don't know how I should behave if shrapnel were bursting over me and knocking the men round me to pieces. But for risks and nerves and fatigues I was all right. That's cheering.

"And there's the empty blue sky and the peaceful village and country scenery, and nothing of war to see except occasional bursts of white smoke, very lazy and quiet, in the distance. But to hear—incessant thunder, shaking buildings and ground, and you and everything; and above, recurrent wailings, very thin and queer, like lost souls, crossing and recrossing in the emptiness— nothing to be seen. Once or twice a lovely glittering aeroplane, very high up, would go over us; and then the shrapnel would be turned on it, and a dozen quiet little curls of white smoke would appear round the creature—the whole thing like a German woodcut, very quaint and peaceful and unreal.

"But the retreat drowned all these impressions. We stole away from the trenches, across half Antwerp, over the Scheldt, and finally entrained in the last train left, at 7.80 next morning. The march through those deserted suburbs, mile on mile, with never a living being, except our rather ferocious-looking sailors stealing sulkily along. The sky was lit by burning villages and houses; and after a bit we got to the land by the river, where the Belgians had let all the petrol out of

the tanks and fired it. Rivers and seas of flames
leaping up hundreds of feet, crowned by black
smoke that covered the entire heavens. It lit up
houses wrecked by shells, dead horses, demol-
ished railway-stations, engines that had been
taken up with their lines and signals, and all
twisted round and pulled out, as a bad child spoils
a toy. . . . . . . The glare was like hell. We
passed on, out of that, across a pontoon bridge
built on boats. Two German spies tried to blow
it up while we were on it. They were caught and
shot. We went on through the dark. The refugees and motor-buses and transport and Belgian
troops grew thicker. After about a thousand
years it was dawn. The motor-buses indicated
that we were bound for Hammersmith, and
might be allowed to see *Potash and Perlmutter*."

Another letter, written on Christmas Day to
Russell Loines of New York, perhaps his greatest friend among his kind American hosts, shows
how deeply the sight of the refugees had moved
him. "I started a long letter to you in August
and September, in my scraps of time; a valuable
letter, full of information about the war and the
state of mind of pacifists and others. The Germans have it now. It went in my luggage to
Antwerp, and there was left. Whether it was
burnt or captured, I can't be sure. But it was

in a tin box, with—damn it!—a lot of my manuscript. And it was fairly heavily shelled.

"I don't know if you heard of my trip to Antwerp. A queer picnic. They say we saved the Belgian army, and most of the valuable things in the town—stores and ammunition, I mean. With luck, we might have kept the line fifty miles forward of where it is. However, we at last got away—most of us. It really was a very mild experience; except the thirty miles march out through the night and the blazing city. Antwerp that night was like several different kinds of hell —the broken houses and dead horses lit up by an infernal glare. The refugees were the worst sight. The German policy of frightfulness had succeeded so well, that out of that city of half a million, when it was decided to surrender Antwerp, not ten thousand would stay. They put their goods on carts, barrows, perambulators, anything. Often the carts had no horses, and they just stayed there in the street, waiting for a miracle. There were all the country refugees, too, from the villages, who had been coming through our lines all day and half the night. I'll never forget that white-faced, endless procession in the night, pressed aside to let the military— us—pass, crawling forward at some hundred yards an hour, quite hopeless, the old men crying, and the women with hard drawn faces. What a crime!—and I gather they've announced their intention of *keeping* Belgium if they can.

"England is remarkable. I wish I had the time to describe it. But this job keeps one so darned tired, and so stupid, that I haven't the words. There are a few people who've been so anti-war before, or so suspicious of diplomacy, that they feel rather out of the national feeling. But it's astonishing to see how the 'intellectuals' have taken on new jobs. No, not astonishing; but impressive. Masefield drills hard in Hampstead, and told me, with some pride, a month ago, that he was a Corporal, and *thought* he was going to be promoted to Sergeant soon. Cornford is no longer the best Greek scholar in Cambridge. He recalled that he was a very good shot in his youth, and is now a Sergeant-Instructor of Musketry. I'm here. My brother is a 2nd Lieutenant in the Post Office Rifles. He was one of three great friends at King's. The second is Intelligence Officer in H.M.S. *Vengeance,* Channel Patrol. The third is buried near Cambrai. Gilbert Murray and Walter Raleigh rise at six every day to line hedgerows in the dark, and 'advance in rushes' across the Oxford meadows.

"Among the other officers in this Division

whom I know are two young Asquiths;[1] an Australian professional pianist[2] who twice won the Diamond Sculls; a New Zealander[3] who was fighting in Mexico and walked 800 miles to the coast to get a boat when he heard of the War; a friend of mine, Denis Browne—Cambridge—who is one of the best young English musicians and an extremely brilliant critic; a youth lately through Eton and Balliol,[4] who is the most brilliant man they've had in Oxford for ten years; a young and very charming American called John Bigelow Dodge, who turned up to 'fight for the right'—I could extend the list. It's all a terrible tragedy. And yet, in its details, it's great fun. And—apart from the tragedy—I've never felt happier or better in my life than in those days in Belgium. And now I've the feeling of anger at a seen wrong—Belgium—to make me happier and more resolved in my work. I know that whatever happens, I'll be doing some good, fighting to prevent *that*."

"I hope to get through," he wrote about the same time to Mrs. Arnold Toynbee. "I'll have such a lot to say and do afterwards. Just now

---

[1] Brigadier-General Arthur Asquith, D.S.O., and his brother Herbert.
[2] F. S. Kelly, killed in action.
[3] Brigadier-General Bernard Freyberg, V.C., D.S.O.
[4] Patrick Shaw-Stewart, killed in action.

I'm rather miserable, because most of my school-friends are wounded, or 'wounded and missing,' or dead. Perhaps our sons will live the better for it all. I knew of yours, I was very glad. It must be good to have a son. When they told us at Dunkirk that we were all going to be killed in Antwerp, if not on the way there, I didn't think much (as I'd expected) what a damned fool I was not to have written more, and done various things better, and been less selfish. I merely thought 'what *Hell* it is that I shan't have any children—any sons.' I thought it over and over, quite furious, for some hours. And we were barely even under fire, in the end!"

"There's a lot to talk about," he told Jacques Raverat, "though I'm rather beyond talking. Yes, we *are* insular. Did you hear of the British private who had been through the fighting from Mons to Ypres, and was asked what he thought of all his experiences? He said, 'What I don't like about this 'ere b—— Europe is all these b—— pictures of Jesus Christ and His relations, behind b—— bits of glawss.'[1] It seems to me to express perfectly that insularity and cheerful atheism which are the chief characteristics of my race.

[1] This was a story of Julian Grenfell's about one of his men, which I had passed on to Rupert.

"All the same, though myself cheerful, insular, and an atheist, I'm largely dissatisfied with the English, just now. The good ones are all right. And it's curiously far away from us (if we haven't the Belgians in memory as I have). But there's a ghastly sort of apathy over half the country. And I really think large numbers of male people don't want to die. Which is odd. I've been praying for a German raid. . . . . . .

"My mind's gone stupid with drill and arranging about the men's food. It's all good fun. I'm rather happy. I've a restful feeling that all's going well and I'm not harming anyone, and probably even doing good. A queer new feeling. The only horror is that I want to marry in a hurry and get a child, before I vanish. . . . . . . There's the question: to ponder in my sleeping-bag, between the thoughts on the attack and calculations about the boots of the platoon. Insoluble: and the weeks slip on. It'll end in my muddling that, as I've muddled everything else."

After they got back from Antwerp, there was a tiresome period of re-shuffling among the different battalions; but by the middle of December, Rupert, Denis Browne, Arthur Asquith, Patrick Shaw-Stewart, Bernard Freyberg and the rest were reunited at Blandford Camp in the

'Hood,' where there were other officers who were
either friends already or belonged to contermin-
ous sets; so that a pleasant family part was soon
established.   The life was strenuous, but not
eventful.   "I spend Christmas," [1] he wrote, "in
looking after drunken stokers.   One of them has
been drunk since 7 a.m.; he neither eats nor
drinks, but dances a complicated step up and
down his hut, singing 'How happy I am, how
happy I am'—a short, fat, inelegant man, in
stockinged feet.   What wonders we are!   There's
no news—occasional scares.   On Wednesday I
(don't tell a soul) started a sonnet.   What a fall!"

The five sonnets called '1914' had been coming
for some time, and were finished at Rugby when
he went there for a few days' leave just after
Christmas.   "These proofs have come," he wrote
from Canford Manor on January 24th.   "My
muse, panting all autumn under halberd and
cuirass, could but falter these syllables through
her vizor.   God, they're in the rough, these five
camp-children—4 and 5 are good though, and
there are phrases in the rest.[2]

---

[1] He had telegraphed just before, to a trusty friend, "Send
mince-pies for sixty men and a few cakes immediately."

[2] "I think *reading* in war-time right enough," he wrote to Miss
Pye from the Mediterranean.   "But writing .equires a longer
period of serenity, a more certainly undisturbed subconsciousness.
If the S.C.'s turbulent, one's draught from it is opaque.   Witness
the first three sonnets."

"Last night I slept between sheets, and this morning I lay an hour in a hot bath, and so was late for a breakfast of pheasant and sausages and the divinest coffee. Now I sit over a great fire of wood in the hall of a house built by Vanbrugh, with a Scuola di Bellini above me, smoking and reading and writing.

"I've been peacefully reading up the country-side all the morning. Where our huts are was an Iberian fort against the Celts—and Celtish against Romans—and Roman against Saxons. . . . Just over the hills is that tower where a young Astronomer watched the stars, and a Lady watched the Astronomer.[1] By Tarrant Hinton, two miles North, George Bubb Dodington lived and reigned and had his salon. In Tarrant Crawford, two miles South, a Queen lies buried. Last week we attacked some of the New Army in Banbury Rings—an ancient fort where Arthur defeated the Saxons in—what year? Where I lay on my belly cursing the stokers for their slowness, Guinevere sat, and wondered if she'd see Arthur and Lancelot return from the fight, or both, or neither, and pictured how they'd look; and then fell a-wondering which, if it came to the point, she'd prefer to see."

"The world's going well," he wrote at this time

[1] See Thomas Hardy's *Two on a Tower*.

to Jacques Raverat: "better than it did when we were younger. And a Frenchman is the one person in the world with something to be proud of, these days."

VII

On January 29th he came to London to recover from a rather bad attack of influenza, staying first at Gray's Inn and then at 10 Downing Street. I saw him for the last time on February 25th, when the King reviewed the Naval Division at Blandford before their departure for the Dardanelles. The secret of where they were going was just out, and everyone was wild with excitement and joy. "It's too wonderful for belief," he wrote to Miss Asquith. "I had not imagined Fate could be so benign. I almost suspect her. Perhaps we shall be held in reserve, out of sight, on a choppy sea, for two months. . . . Yet even that! . . . But I'm filled with confident and glorious hopes. I've been looking at the maps. Do you think *perhaps* the fort on the Asiatic corner will want quelling, and we'll land and come at it from behind, and they'll make a sortie and meet us on the plains of Troy? It seems to me strategically so possible. Shall we have a Hospital Base (and won't you manage it?) on Lesbos? Will Hero's Tower crumble under the 15″ guns? Will the sea be polyphloisbic and wine-dark and unvintageable? Shall I loot mosaics from St. Sophia, and Turkish Delight, and carpets? Should we be a Turning Point in History? Oh God!

"I've never been quite so happy in my life, I think. Not quite so pervasively happy; like a stream flowing entirely to one end. I suddenly realise that the ambition of my life has been—since I was two—to go on a military expedition against Constantinople. And when I *thought* I was hungry or sleepy or aching to write a poem —*that* was what I really, blindly, wanted. This is nonsense. Good-night. I'm very tired with equipping my platoon."

They sailed from Avonmouth in the *Grantully Castle* on February 28th. "Four days out," he dated his next letter to Miss Asquith. "All day we've been just out of sight of land, thirty or forty miles away—out of sight, but in smell. There was something earthy in the air, and warm —like the consciousness of a presence in the dark —the wind had something Andalusian in it. It wasn't that wall of scent and invisible blossom and essential spring that knocks you flat, quite suddenly, as you've come round some unseen corner in the atmosphere, fifty miles out from a

South Sea Island; but it *was* the good smell of land—and of Spain, too! And Spain I've never seen, and never shall see, may be. All day I sat and strained my eyes to see over the horizon orange-groves and Moorish buildings, and dark-eyed beauties and guitars, and fountains, and a golden darkness. But the curve of the world lay between us. Do you know Jan [Masefield]'s favourite story—told very melodiously with deep-voice reverence—about Columbus? Columbus wrote a diary (which Jan reads) and described the coast of America as he found it—*the* divinest place in the world. 'It was only like the Paradise of the Saints of God'—and then he remembered that there was *one* place equal to it, the place where he was born—and goes on 'or like the gardens of Andalusia in the spring.'"

He wrote to me from 'North of Tunis' on March 7th. "It seems ages ago since we said good-bye to you on our mottled parade-ground. We've had rather a nice voyage; a bit unsteady the first day (when I was sick) and to-day; otherwise very smooth and delicious. There has been a little, not much, to do. I've read most of *Turkey in Europe*. But what with parades and the reading of military books, I've not written anything. Anyway, my mind's always a blank at sea.

"For two days we've been crawling along the African Coast, observing vast tawny mountains, with white villages on this side of them and white peaks beyond. The sea has been a jewel, and sunset and dawn divine blazes of colour. It's all too ridiculously peaceful for one to believe anything but that we're a—rather odd—lot of tourists, seeing the Mediterranean and bent on enjoyment. War seems infinitely remote; and even the reason, foreseeing Gallipoli, yet admits that there are many blue days to come, and the Cyclades. . . . . . .

"I can well see that life might be great fun; and I can well see death might be an admirable solution. . . . . . .

"In a fortnight, the quarter million Turks."

I think these words on the prospect of living or dying represent his normal state of mind; and that he had nothing which could justly be called a *presentiment* of death. "This is very odd," was the beginning of a letter which he wrote for me in case he died. "But I suppose I must imagine my non-existence, and make a few arrangements." He certainly spoke to some people as though he were sure of not coming back; but no one can read the letters I have printed without seeing what a creature of moods he was; and it was always his way to dramatise the future.

There was a vivid realisation of the possibility
—I believe that was all.[1]

He spoke in the letter I have just quoted of a
wish he had expressed to his mother (which she
has carried out), that any money he left, and any
profits from his books, should be divided between
three of his brother poets. "If I can set them
free to any extent," he told her, "to write the
poetry and plays and books they want to, my
death will bring more gain than loss." The three
were Lascelles Abercrombie, Walter de la Mare,
and Wilfrid Gibson.[2]

---

[1] The preoccupation with the idea of death, shown in his poems
from the first, has often been noticed. When I looked through
his copy of Aristophanes, I was struck by a heavy triple mark
which he had put against two lines of the *Frogs*—almost the only
passage he had marked at all:

τεθνηκόσιν γὰρ ἔλεγεν , ὦ μοχθηρὲ σύ,
οἷς οὐδὲ τρὶς λέγοντες ἐξικνούμεθα.

"Aye, but he's speaking to the dead, you knave,
Who cannot hear us though we call them thrice."
(B. B. Rogers' translation.)

This may have suggested the phrase about the 'unanswering dead'
in *Ambarvalia*, which occurs again in a fragment, probably written
in 1914:—

"We have told you the last lies, unanswering Dead.
Farewell, we have said,
Knowing the Dead fare neither ill nor well."

[2] Mrs. Brooke included in this bequest the amount of the Howland Memorial Prize, the first award of which was unanimously
made to her son in 1916, after his death, by the Committee of the
Corporation of Yale University. The prize is given "in recognition
of some achievement of marked distinction in the field of literature
or fine arts or the science of government; and an important factor
in the selection is the idealistic element in the recipient's work."
Mr. Charles Howland wrote to Mrs. Brooke announcing the

"We had a very amusing evening in Malta,"
he wrote to his mother on March 12th. "Our
boat got in one afternoon almost last of the lot.
We were allowed ashore from 5 to midnight.
Oc,[1] Denis and I drove around in a funny little
carriage, and looked at the views. It's a very
lovely place; very like Verona or any Italian
town, but rather cleaner and more Southern.
There was a lovely Mediterranean sunset and
evening, and the sky and sea were filled with
colours. The odd and pleasant thing was the
way we kept running into people we knew and
hadn't expected to meet. First there were people in all the other battalions, who had come on
by other boats. Then we found 'Cardy' [Lionel]
Montagu, E.S.M.'s brother, staring at the Cathedral. Then Cherry, who used to be in the Anson
with us, a nice chap, and he dined with us; and
in, at the end of dinner, came Patrick Shaw-
Stewart (of this Battalion) with Charles Lister,
who was dragged in absolutely at the last mo-

award: "You must have known already by many avenues of the
feeling about him in the United States—of the sense of tenderness
for his youth, of the attitude of possession of him jointly with
Englishmen as one of the Masters of Song in our common tongue;
and indeed that he typifies the nobility of sacrifice for a cause that
is ours as well as yours."

The lecture, which by the terms of the gift was due from the
prizewinner, was delivered at Yale by Walter de la Mare in his
stead.

[1] Arthur Asquith.

ment because he is supposed to know Turkish, and is with the Divisional Staff. Before dinner, as I was buying buttons in a little shop, in walked George Peel! And after dinner, at a nice little opera, everyone I knew seemed to appear, in khaki, all very cheerful and gay. Lots of people who we thought were going to be left behind had been able to get out at the last moment, and pounced on us from behind boxes or out of stalls. The Maltese *élite* who were there must have been puzzled at the noise."

From Malta they went on to Lemnos; "the *loveliest* place in the evening sun," he wrote, "softly white, grey, silver-white buildings, some very old, some new, round a great harbour—all very Southern; like an Italian town in silver-point, livable and serene, with a sea and sky of opal and pearl and faint gold around. It was nearer than any place I've ever seen to what a Greek must have witnessed when he sailed into a Greek coast-city."

Here there was an alarum, but not an excursion, as appears from a letter to Miss Cox, dated "Somewhere (some way from the front) March 19th." "The other day we—some of us—were told that we sailed next day to make a landing. A few thousand of us. Off we stole that night through the phosphorescent Aegean, scribbling farewell letters, and snatching periods of excited dream-broken sleep. At four we rose, buckled on our panoply, hung ourselves with glasses, compasses, periscopes, revolvers, food, and the rest, and had a stealthy large breakfast. *That was a mistake.* It's ruinous to load up one's belly four or five hours before it expects it—it throws the machinery out of gear for a week. I felt extremely ill the rest of that day.

"We paraded in silence under paling stars along the sides of the ship. The darkness on the sea was full of scattered flashing lights, hinting at our fellow-transports and the rest. Slowly the sky became warm and green, and the sea opal. Everyone's face looked drawn and ghastly. If we landed, my company was to be the first to land. . . . We made out that we were only a mile or two from a dim shore. I was seized with an agony of remorse that I hadn't taught my platoon a thousand things more energetically and competently. The light grew. The shore looked to be crammed with Fate, and was ominously silent. One man thought he saw a camel through his glasses. . . .

"There were some hours of silence.

"About seven, someone said, 'We're going home.' We dismissed the stokers, who said, quietly, 'When's the next battle?', and disempanoplied, and had another breakfast. If we were a 'feint,' or if it was too rough to land, or in general, what little part we blindly played, we never knew, and shall not. Still, we did our bit, not ignobly, I trust. We did not see the enemy. We did not fire at them; nor they at us. It seemed improbable they saw us. One of B Company—she was rolling very slightly—was sick on parade. Otherwise, no casualties. A notable battle.

"Later. We're off to Egypt: for repose. For —I imagine—a month at least. What a life! Another campaign over!"

On March 27th they arrived at Port Said, and he went for three days' leave with Arthur Asquith and Patrick Shaw-Stewart to Cairo, where they saw the Sphinx and the Pyramids, rode about on camels, and bought things in the bazaars.

Sir Ian Hamilton came to Port Said to review the Naval Division on April 3rd, and offered him a post on his staff. "I saw Rupert Brooke," he wrote to me, "lying down under a shelter, rather off colour, poor boy. He had got a touch of the sun the previous day. It was nothing, and essentially he was looking in first-class physical condition. He very naturally would like to see this first adventure through with his own men;

after that I think he would like to come to me.
It was very natural, and I quite understand it—
I should have answered the same in his case had
I been offered a staff billet." Rupert never
mentioned this offer to his brother-officers. "The
first day I was sick," he wrote to his mother,
"before I got out of camp—was the day when
our new G.O.C.-in-Chief—you'll know who that
is—reviewed us. I'd met him once or twice in
London. He came to see me after the review
and talked for a bit. He offered me a sort of
galloper-aide-de-camp job on his staff: but I
shan't take it. Anyhow, not now, not till this
present job's over; afterwards, if I've had enough
of the regimental officer's work, I might like it."
"But it's really so jolly," he wrote to me on the
same occasion, "being with Oc and Denis and
Charles [Lister] and Patrick and Kelly, that it'd
have to be very tempting company to persuade
me to give it up."

That evening he joined Patrick Shaw-Stewart,
who had the same illness, at the Casino Hotel.
"Then began nearly a week of comic alternations
and vicissitudes in our humiliating complaint,"
Shaw-Stewart wrote to me. "The companionship in our two little beds was very close, but
limited by our mental state, which owing to starvation was—for me—complete vacuity. So we

just lay opposite and grew our little beards, mine red, his golden brown, and made our little jokes at one another—very good ones, I can't help thinking. Altogether, if it hadn't been for the starvation and the uncomfortable beds and the terrible difficulty of making the Italian waiter understand (R. did better with gesticulatory English than I with Italian, which made me furious) it was the best period of the war for me. We were turned out rather quickly. On the Friday morning, April 9th, we were ordered to be aboard that evening if we were well enough, which of course we both said we were. In my case there was no doubt I was: in R.'s I think it was doubtful, and Colonel Quilter rather urged him to stay behind if he still felt queer, but of course it would have been a difficult thing (morally) to do. So we both went on board and stuck to our cabins for a day or two, R. emerging later than me. Just at this time he seemed really pretty well (as well as at Blandford, which I think for him probably wasn't so very well) but a little listless."

Rupert himself wrote to Miss Asquith the day he left the hotel, "Anyhow here I am, well up on that difficult slope that leads from arrowroot, past chicken broth, by rice puddings, to eggs in

milk, and so to eggs, and boiled fish, and finally
(they say) chicken and fruit and even real meat.
But that is still beyond the next crest. On! on!
But while I shall be well, I think, for our first
thrust into the fray, I shall be able to give my
Turk, at the utmost, a kitten's tap. A diet of
arrowroot doesn't build up violence. I am as
weak as a pacifist."

About the same time he wrote to Lascelles
Abercrombie: "The Sun-God (he, the Song-
God) distinguished one of his most dangerous
rivals since Marsyas among the x thousand
tanned and dirty men blown suddenly on these
his special coasts a few days or weeks ago. He
unslung his bow. . . . I lie in an hotel, cool at
length, with wet cloths on my head and less than
nothing in my belly. Sunstroke is a bloody affair. It breaks very suddenly the fair harmonies
of the body and the soul. I'm lying recovering
from it, living faintly on arrowroot and rice-pud-
dings and milk; passing from dream to dream,
all faint and tasteless and pure as arrowroot itself. I shall be all right in time for the fighting,
I hope and believe.

"*Later* (*at sea*). I know now what a campaign
is. I had a suspicion from Antwerp. It is continual crossing from one place to another, and

back, over dreamlike seas: anchoring, or halting, in the oddest places, for no one knows or quite cares how long: drifting on, at last, to some other equally unexpected, equally out of the way, equally odd spot: for all the world like a bottle in some corner of the bay at a seaside resort. Somewhere, sometimes, there is fighting. Not for us. In the end, no doubt, our apparently aimless course will drift us through, or anchor us in, a blaze of war, quite suddenly; and as suddenly swirl us out again. Meanwhile, the laziest loitering lotus-day I idled away as a wanderer in the South Seas was a bustle of decision and purpose compared to a campaign.

"One just hasn't, though, the time and detachment to write, I find. But I've been collecting a few words, detaching lines from the ambient air, collaring one or two of the golden phrases that a certain wind blows from (will the Censor let me say?) Olympus, across these purple seas."

VIII

Of the 'golden phrases,' only the merest fragments remain. He must have made up more in his head than he wrote down, for his last letter

to me implies a good deal more than there is.
"The first few days afloat I was still convalescent.
So I could lie in my bunk and read and write in
a delicious solitude all day. I actually *did* jot
down a line or two. Nothing yet complete (except a song, worthless alone, for Denis to put
lovely notes around); but a sonnet or two almost
done; and the very respectable and shapely
skeleton of an ode-threnody. All of which shall
travel to you if and when they are done. . . . . . .
I must go and censor my platoon's letters. My
long poem is to be about the existence—and non-
locality—of England. And it contains the line
—'In Avons of the heart her rivers run.' Lovely,
isn't it?"

There is only a small black note-book, from
which I will put together what I can. There will
be found in the appendix the little song called
The Dance, mentioned in the letter; and a fragment which is almost his only attempt at blank
verse—though even here rhyme steals in towards
the end. Here are the scraps which seem to belong to the 'ode-threnody' on England:

> All things are written in the mind.
> There the sure hills have station; and the wind
> Blows   in that placeless air.
> And there the white and golden birds go flying;
> And the stars wheel and shine; and woods are fair;

The light upon the snow is there;
                   and in that nowhere move
The trees and hills [1] and waters that we love.

And she for whom we die, she the undying
Mother of men
England!

      * * *

In Avons of the heart her rivers run.

      * * *

She is with all we have loved and found and known,
Closed in the little nowhere of the brain.
Only, of all our dreams,
Not the poor heap of   dust and stone,
This local earth, set in terrestrial streams,
Not this man, giving all for gold,
Nor that who has found evil good, nor these
Blind millions, bought and sold . . .

      * * *

She is not here, or now—
She is here, and now, yet nowhere—
We gave her birth, who bore us—
Our wandering feet have sought, but never found her—
She is built a long way off—
She, though all men be traitors, not betrayed—
Whose soil is love, and her stars justice, she—
Gracious with flowers,
And robed   and glorious in the sea. [2]

      * * *

[1] The word 'hands' is written here, I think, by mistake for 'hills.' Compare 'the trees and waters and the hills' in his early poem, *The Charm.*

[2] This last set of lines, or rather jottings, is not written as if they were meant to be consecutive.

She was in his eyes, but he could not see her.
And he was England, but he knew her not.

There are fragments of other poems; two about
the expedition:

They say Achilles in the darkness stirred,
And   Hector, his old enemy,
Moved the great shades that were his limbs. They
     heard
More than Olympian thunder on the sea.

*　*　*

Death and Sleep
Bear many a young Sarpedon home.

And this, headed 'Queen Elizabeth':

And Priam and his fifty sons
Wake all amazed, and hear the guns,
     And shake for Troy again.

Then there is this:—

'When Nobby tried,' the stokers say,
  'To stop a shrapnel with his belly,
He   away,
  He left a lump of bleeding jelly.'
But *he* went out, did Nobby Clark [1]
Upon the illimitable dark,
Out of the fields where soldiers stray,
  Beyond parades, beyond reveille.

[1] All sailors whose name is Clark are nick-named Nobby. No
one knows why.

This is for one of the sonnets:

The poor scrap of a song that some man tried
Down in the troop-decks forrard, brought again
The day you sang it first, on a hill-side,
With April in the wind and in the brain.
And the woods were gold; and youth was in our hands.

* * *

Oh lovers parted,
Oh all you lonely over all the world,
You that look out at morning empty-hearted,
Or you, all night turning uncomforted

* * *

Would God, would God, you could be comforted.

* * *

Eyes that weep,
And a long time for love; and, after, sleep.

There are lines of a poem about evening, in which he recurs to the hares in the Grantchester cornfields:

And daylight, like a dust, sinks through the air,
And drifting, golds the ground . . .
A lark,
A voice in heaven, in fading deeps of light,
Drops, at length, home.

* * *

A wind of night, shy as the young hare
That steals even now out of the corn to play,
Stirs the pale river once, and creeps away.

And of an elegy:

The feet that ran with mine have found their goal,
The eyes that met my eyes have looked on night.
The firm limbs are no more; gone back to earth,
Easily mingling . . .
                    What he is yet,
Not living, lives, hath place in a few minds . . .

                                        He wears
The ungathered blossom of quiet; stiller he
Than a deep well at noon, or lovers met;
Than sleep, or the heart after wrath. He is
The silence following great words of peace.

That is all.

On the 17th of April they landed at Scyros.
Arthur Asquith described it to his sister before
anything had happened: "This island is more
mountainous than Lemnos, and more sparsely in-
habited. It is like one great rock-garden of
white and pinkish-white marble, with small red
poppies and every sort of wildflower; in the
gorges ilex, dwarf holly, and occasional groups of
olives; and everywhere the smell of thyme (or is
it sage? or wild mint?). Our men kill adders
and have fun with big tortoises. The water near
the shore, where the bottom is white marble, is
more beautifully green and blue than I have ever
seen it anywhere."

Here then, in the island where Theseus was buried, and whence the young Achilles and the young Pyrrhus were called to Troy, Rupert Brooke died and was buried on Friday, the 23rd of April, the day of Shakespeare and of St. George.

He seemed quite well till Tuesday the 20th, when there was a Divisional Field-day, and he went to bed tired immediately after dinner. On Wednesday he stayed in bed with pains in his back and head; and a swelling on his lip; but no anxiety was felt till the evening, when he had a temperature of 103. Next morning he was much worse; the swelling had increased, and a consultation was held. The diagnosis was acute blood-poisoning, and all hope was given up. It was decided to move him to the French hospital-ship *Duguay-Trouin* which happened to be at Scyros. When he was told this, his one anxiety was lest he should have difficulty in rejoining his battalion. They reassured him, and he seemed to be content. Soon afterwards he became comatose; and there does not seem to have been any moment when he can have realised that he was dying. The rest of the story shall be told in the words of the letter which Denis Browne wrote me on the 25th from the transport.

"In less than half an hour we had carried him

down into a pinnace and taken him straight aboard the *Duguay-Trouin*. They put him in the best cabin, on the sun-deck. Everything was very roomy and comfortable; they had every modern appliance and the surgeons did all that they possibly could.[1] Oc and I left him about 6 when we could do nothing more, and went to the *Franconia,* where we sent a wireless message to the Admiralty.[2] Next morning Oc and I went over to see what we could do, and found him much weaker. There was nothing to be done, as he was quite unconscious and they were busy trying all the devices they could think of to give him ease. Not that he was suffering, for he was barely conscious all Thursday (he just said 'Hallo' when I went to lift him out into the pinnace), and on Friday he was not conscious at all up to the very last, and felt no pain whatever. At 2 the head surgeon told me he was sinking. Oc went off to see about arrangements, and I sat with Rupert. At 4 o'clock he became weaker,

---

[1] "I do want you to feel," Browne wrote to Mrs. Brooke, "that nothing was left undone that could alleviate his condition or prolong his life. Nothing, however, all the doctors, French and English, assured me, could have helped him to fight his disease, except a strong constitution. And his was so enfeebled by illness as to make the contest an unequal one. They gave us hardly any hope from the first."

[2] The telegrams were received as if from Lemnos, and as there was no reason to suppose otherwise it was assumed, and published, that he had died there.

and at 4.46 he died, with the sun shining all round his cabin, and the cool sea-breeze blowing through the door and the shaded windows. No one could have wished a quieter or a calmer end than in that lovely bay, shielded by the mountains and fragrant with sage and thyme.[1]

"We buried him the same evening in an olive-grove where he had sat with us on Tuesday—one of the loveliest places on this earth, with grey-green olives round him, one weeping above his head; the ground covered with flowering sage, bluish-grey, and smelling more delicious than any flower I know. The path up to it from the sea is narrow and difficult and very stony; it runs by the bed of a dried-up torrent. We had to post men with lamps every twenty yards to guide the bearers. He was carried up from the boat by his A Company petty officers, led by his platoon-sergeant Saunders; and it was with enormous difficulty that they got the coffin up the narrow way. The journey of a mile took two hours. It was not till 11 that I saw them coming (I had gone up to choose the place, and with Freyberg and Charles Lister I turned the sods of his grave; we had some of his platoon to dig). First came one of his men carrying a great white wooden

---

[1] This sentence is from the letter to Mrs. Brooke.

cross with his name painted on it in black; then
the firing-party, commanded by Patrick; and
then the coffin, followed by our officers, and General Paris and one or two others of the Brigade.
Think of it all under a clouded moon, with the
three mountains [1] around and behind us, and
those divine scents everywhere. We lined his
grave with all the flowers we could find, and
Quilter set a wreath of olive on the coffin. The
funeral service was very simply said by the Chap-
lain, and after the Last Post the little lamp-lit
procession went once again down the narrow path
to the sea.

"Freyberg, Oc, I, Charles and Cleg [Kelly]
stayed behind and covered the grave with great
pieces of white marble which were lying everywhere about. Of the cross at the head you know;
it was the large one that headed the procession.
On the back of it our Greek interpreter wrote in
pencil:

ἐνθάδε κεῖται
ὁ δοῦλος τοῦ Θεοῦ
ἀνθυπολοχαγὸς τοῦ
Ἀγγλικοῦ ναυτικοῦ
ἀποθανὼν ὑπὲρ τῆς
ἀπελευθερώσεως τῆς
Κων' πόλεως ἀπὸ
τῶν Τουρκῶν.[2]

[1] Their names are Paphko, Komaro, and Khokilas.
[2] Here lies the servant of God, Sub-Lieutenant in the English
Navy, who died for the deliverance of Constantinople from the
Turks.

At his feet was a small wooden cross sent by his platoon. We could not see the grave again, as we sailed from Scyros next morning at 6."

The same friend wrote to Mrs. Brooke: "No words of mine can tell you the sorrow of those whom he has left behind him here. No one of us knew him without loving him, whether they knew him for ten years, as I did, or for a couple of months as others. His brother officers and his men mourn him very deeply. But those who knew him chiefly as a poet of the rarest gifts, the brightest genius, know that the loss is not only yours and ours, but the world's. And beyond his genius there was that infinitely lovable soul, that stainless heart whose earthly death can only be the beginning of a true immortality.

"To his friends Rupert stood for something so much purer, greater, and nobler than ordinary men that his loss seems more explicable than theirs. He has gone to where he came from; but if anyone left the world richer by passing through it, it was he."

Next morning the *Grantully Castle* sailed for the Gallipoli Peninsula. Within six weeks, of the officers named in Denis Browne's letter, he and Colonel Quilter were dead, and all but one of the others had been wounded. Kelly, Lister, and Shaw-Stewart have since been killed.

Winston Churchill wrote in the *Times* of April 26th: "Rupert Brooke is dead. A telegram from the Admiral at Lemnos tells us that this life has closed at the moment when it seemed to have reached its springtime. A voice had become audible, a note had been struck, more true, more thrilling, more able to do justice to the nobility of our youth in arms engaged in this present war, than any other—more able to express their thoughts of self-surrender, and with a power to carry comfort to those who watched them so intently from afar. The voice has been swiftly stilled. Only the echoes and the memory remain; but they will linger.

"During the last few months of his life, months of preparation in gallant comradeship and open air, the poet-soldier told with all the simple force of genius the sorrow of youth about to die, and the sure triumphant consolations of a sincere and valiant spirit. He expected to die; he was willing to die for the dear England whose beauty and majesty he knew; and he advanced towards the brink in perfect serenity, with absolute conviction of the rightness of his country's cause, and a heart devoid of hate for fellow-men.

"The thoughts to which he gave expression in the very few incomparable war sonnets which he has left behind will be shared by many thousands of young men moving resolutely and blithely forward into this, the hardest, the cruellest, and the least-rewarded of all the wars that men have fought. They are a whole history and revelation of Rupert Brooke himself. Joyous, fearless, versatile, deeply instructed, with classic symmetry of mind and body, he was all that one would wish England's noblest sons to be in days when no sacrifice but the most precious is acceptable, and the most precious is that which is most freely proffered."

.   .   .   .   .   .

"Coming from Alexandria yesterday," Denis Browne wrote to me on June 2nd, two days before his own death, "we passed Rupert's island at sunset. The sea and sky in the East were grey and misty; but it stood out in the West, black and immense, with a crimson glowing halo round it. Every colour had come into the sea and sky to do him honour; and it seemed that the island must ever be shining with his glory that we buried there."

APPENDIX

NOTE

The Appendix contains: (1) the only two coherent fragments found in the notebook which he used in the last month of his life (see Memoir, page 175); a little song, written, I think, on his travels; and a poem, dating probably from 1912, which for some reason he left unrevised, but which I print for the sake of the characteristic image in the first stanza: (2) a few 'lighter' poems which I dare say he would have printed on their merits if he had published a volume in which they would not have been out of key. Two of these, the "Letter to a Live Poet" and "The Little Dog's Day," were written for *Westminster Gazette* competitions, in which they won prizes.

E. M.

FRAGMENT

I strayed about the deck, an hour, to-night
Under a cloudy moonless sky; and peeped
In at the windows, watched my friends at table,
Or playing cards, or standing in the doorway,
Or coming out into the darkness. Still
No one could see me.

                    I would have thought of them
—Heedless, within a week of battle—in pity,
Pride in their strength and in the weight and firmness
And link'd beauty of bodies, and pity that
This gay machine of splendour 'ld soon be broken,
Thought little of, pashed, scattered. . . .

                        Only, always,
I could but see them—against the lamplight—pass
Like coloured shadows, thinner than filmy glass,
Slight bubbles, fainter than the wave's faint light,
That broke to phosphorus out in the night,
Perishing things and strange ghosts—soon to die
To other ghosts—this one, or that, or I.

April, 1915.

THE DANCE

A Song

As the Wind, and as the Wind,
In a corner of the way,
Goes stepping, stands twirling,
Invisibly, comes whirling,
Bows before, and skips behind,
In a grave, an endless play—

So my Heart, and so my Heart,
Following where your feet have gone,
Stirs dust of old dreams there;
He turns a toe; he gleams there,
Treading you a dance apart.
But you see not. You pass on.

April, 1915.

SONG

The way of love was thus.
He was born one winter morn
With hands delicious,
And it was well with us.

Love came our quiet way,
Lit pride in us, and died in us,
All in a winter's day.
There is no more to say.

1918 (?).

SOMETIMES EVEN NOW ...

Sometimes even now I may
Steal a prisoner's holiday,
Slip, when all is worst, the bands,
  Hurry back, and duck beneath
Time's old tyrannous groping hands,
  Speed away with laughing breath
Back to all I'll never know,
Back to you, a year ago.

Truant there from Time and Pain,
What I had, I find again:
Sunlight in the boughs above,
  Sunlight in your hair and dress,
The Hands too proud for all but Love,
  The Lips of utter kindliness,
The Heart of bravery swift and clean
  Where the best was safe, I knew,
And laughter in the gold and green,
  And song, and friends, and ever you
With smiling and familiar eyes,
  You—but friendly: you—but true.

And Innocence accounted wise,
  And Faith the fool, the pitiable.
Love so rare, one would swear
  All of earth for ever well—
Careless lips and flying hair,
  And little things I may not tell.

It does but double the heart-ache
When I wake, when I wake.

1912 (?).

SONNET: IN TIME OF REVOLT

The Thing must End. I am no boy! I AM
  No BOY! ! being twenty-one. Uncle, you make
  A great mistake, a very great mistake,
In chiding me for letting slip a 'Damn!'
What's more, you called me 'Mother's one ewe lamb,'
  Bade me 'refrain from swearing—for *her* sake—
  Till I'm grown up' . . . —By God! I think you take
Too much upon you, Uncle William!

You say I am your brother's only son.
I know it. And, 'What of it?' I reply.
My heart's resolvéd. *Something must be done.*
So shall I curb, so baffle, so suppress
This too avuncular officiousness,
Intolerable consanguinity.

   January, 1908.

A LETTER TO A LIVE POET

Sir, since the last Elizabethan died,
Or, rather, that more Paradisal muse,
Blind with much light, passed to the light more glorious
Or deeper blindness, no man's hand, as thine,
Has, on the world's most noblest chord of song,
Struck certain magic strains. Ears satiate
With the clamorous, timorous whisperings of to-day,

Thrilled to perceive once more the spacious voice
And serene utterance of old. We heard
—With rapturous breath half-held, as a dreamer dreams
Who dares not know it dreaming, lest he wake—
The odorous, amorous style of poetry,
The melancholy knocking of those lines,
The long, low soughing of pentameters,
—Or the sharp of rhyme as a bird's cry—
And the innumerable truant polysyllables
Multitudinously twittering like a bee.
Fulfilled our hearts were with that music then,
And all the evenings sighed it to the dawn,
And all the lovers heard it from all the trees.
All of the accents upon all the norms!
—And ah! the stress on the penultimate!
We never knew blank verse could have such feet.

Where is it now? Oh, more than ever, now,
I sometimes think no poetry is read
Save where some sepultured Cæsura bled,
Royally incarnadining all the line.
Is the imperial iamb laid to rest,
And the young trochee, having done enough?

Ah! turn again! Sing so to us, who are sick
Of seeming-simple rhymes, bizarre emotions,
Decked in the simple verses of the day,
Infinite meaning in a little gloom,
Irregular thoughts in stanzas regular,
Modern despair in antique metres, myths
Incomprehensible at evening,
And symbols that mean nothing in the dawn.

The slow lines swell. The new style sighs. The Celt
Moans round with many voices.

God! to see

Gaunt anapæsts stand up out of the verse,
Combative accents, stress where no stress should be,
Spondee on spondee, iamb on choriamb,
The thrill of all the tribrachs in the world,
And all the vowels rising to the E!
To hear the blessed mutter of those verbs,
Conjunctions passionate toward each other's arms,
And epithets like amaranthine lovers
Stretching luxuriously to the stars,
All prouder pronouns than the dawn, and all
The thunder of the trumpets of the noun!

January, 1911.

FRAGMENT ON PAINTERS

There is an evil which that Race attaints
Who represent God's World with oily paints,
Who mock the Universe, so rare and sweet,
With spots of colour on a canvas sheet,
Defile the Lovely and insult the Good
By scrawling upon little bits of wood.
They'd snare the moon, and catch the immortal sun
With madder brown and pale vermilion,
Entrap an English evening's magic hush . . . .

THE TRUE BEATITUDE

They say, when the Great Prompter's hand shall ring
  Down the last curtain upon earth and sea,
  All the Good Mimes will have eternity
To praise their Author, worship love and sing;
Or to the walls of Heaven wandering
  Look down on those damned for a fretful d——,
  Mock them (all theologians agree
On this reward for virtue), laugh, and fling

New sulphur on the sin-incarnadined . . .
  Ah, Love! still temporal, and still atmospheric,
    Teleologically unperturbed,
We share a peace by no divine divined,
  An earthly garden hidden from any cleric,
    Untrodden of God, by no Eternal curbed.

1913.

SONNET REVERSED

Hand trembling towards hand; the amazing lights
Of heart and eye. They stood on supreme heights.

Ah, the delirious weeks of honeymoon!
  Soon they returned, and, after strange adventures,
Settled at Balham by the end of June.
  Their money was in Can. Pacs. B. Debentures,

And in Antofagastas. Still he went
  Cityward daily; still she did abide
At home. And both were really quite content
  With work and social pleasures. Then they died.
They left three children (besides George, who drank):
  The eldest Jane, who married Mr. Bell,
William, the head-clerk in the County Bank,
  And Henry, a stock-broker, doing well.

LULWORTH, 1, *January*, 1911.

THE LITTLE DOG'S DAY

All in the town were still asleep,
When the sun came up with a shout and leap.
In the lonely streets unseen by man,
A little dog danced. And the day began.

All his life he'd been good, as far as he could,
And the poor little beast had done all that he should.
But this morning he swore, by Odin and Thor
And the Canine Valhalla—he'd stand it no more!

So his prayer he got granted—to do just what he wanted,
Prevented by none, for the space of one day.
'*Jam incipiebo,*[1] *sedere facebo,*'[2]
In dog-Latin he quoth, '*Euge! sophos! hurray!*'

[1] Now we're off.
[2] *I'll* make them sit up.

He fought with the he-dogs, and winked at the she-dogs,
A thing that had never been *heard* of before.
'For the stigma of gluttony, I care not a button!' he
Cried, and ate all he could swallow—and more.

He took sinewy lumps from the shins of old frumps,
And mangled the errand-boys—when he could get 'em.
He shammed furious *rabies*,[1] and bit all the babies,[1]
And followed the cats up the trees, and then ate 'em!

They thought 'twas the devil was holding a revel,
And sent for the parson to drive him away;
For the town never knew such a hullabaloo
As that little dog raised—till the end of that day.

When the blood-red sun had gone burning down,
And the lights were lit in the little town,
Outside, in the gloom of the twilight grey,
The little dog died when he'd had his day.

July, 1907.

[1] Pronounce either to suit rhyme.

cА.

Jw

Lightning Source UK Ltd.
Milton Keynes UK
UKHW032047201120
373782UK00008B/1734